JOHN BETJEMAN EARLY POEMS

COMPILED BY
The Earl of Birkenhead

ISIS Large Print
Oxford   New York

First published in Great Britain
by John Murray Ltd.,
50 Albemarle Street, London W1X 4BD

Published in Large Print 1986 by Clio Press Ltd.,
55 St Thomas' St., Oxford OX1 1JG,
by arrangement with John Murray Ltd.

British Library Cataloguing in Publication Data

Betjeman, John
    John Betjeman's early poems.
    I. Title   II. Birkenhead, Frederick Winston
    Furneaux Smith. *Earl of*
    821'.912   PR6003.E77

ISBN 1-85089-095-1

Phototypeset, printed and bound by
Unwin Brothers Limited, Old Woking, Surrey.
Cover designed by CGS Studios, Cheltenham.

CONTENTS

MOUNT ZION (1932)

CONTINUAL DEW (1937)

OLD LIGHTS FOR NEW CHANCELS
(1940)

NEW BATS IN OLD BELFRIES (1945)

SELECTED POEMS (1948)

ACKNOWLEDGEMENTS

Grateful acknowledgement is made to the Editors of *Punch*, *The London Magazine*, *The New Yorker*, *Harper's Bazaar*, *The Saturday Book*, *The Cornhill*, *The Atlantic Monthly*, *Encounter*, *The Observer*, *Vogue*, *Weekend Telegraph* and *The Philbeach Quarterly*.

The author is grateful to his friends John Hanbury Angus Sparrow, Lord Birkenhead and Thomas Edward Neil Driberg. The first made and introduced the original selection for *Selected Poems*; the second advised on the first edition of *Collected Poems* and the third corrected grammar and punctuation, and changed some lines for the better.

Death in Leamington

She died in the upstairs bedroom
  By the light of the ev'ning star
That shone through the plate glass
    window
  From over Leamington Spa.

Beside her the lonely crochet
  Lay patiently and unstirred,
But the fingers that would have
    work'd it
  Were dead as the spoken word.

And Nurse came in with the tea-things
  Breast high 'mid the stands and chairs—
But Nurse was alone with her own little
    soul,
  And the things were alone with theirs.

She bolted the big round window,
  She let the blinds unroll,
She set a match to the mantle,
  She covered the fire with coal.

And "Tea!" she said in a tiny voice
  "Wake up! It's nearly *five*."
Oh! Chintzy, chintzy cheeriness,
  Half dead and half alive!

Do you know that the stucco is peeling?
  Do you know that the heart will stop?
From those yellow Italianate arches
  Do you hear the plaster drop?

Nurse looked at the silent bedstead,
  At the gray, decaying face,
As the calm of a Leamington ev'ning
  Drifted into the place.

She moved the table of bottles
  Away from the bed to the wall;
And tiptoeing gently over the stairs
  Turned down the gas in the hall.

Hymn

The Church's Restoration
  In eighteen-eighty-three
Has left for contemplation
  Not what there used to be.
How well the ancient woodwork
  Looks round the Rect'ry hall,
Memorial of the good work
  Of him who plann'd it all.

He who took down the pew-ends
  And sold them anywhere
But kindly spared a few ends
  Work'd up into a chair.
O worthy persecution
  Of dust! O hue divine!
O cheerful substitution,
  Thou varnishéd pitch-pine!

Church furnishing! Church furnishing!
  Sing art and crafty praise!
He gave the brass for burnishing
  He gave the thick red baize,
He gave the new addition,

Pull'd down the dull old aisle,
—To pave the sweet transition
He gave th' encaustic tile.

Of marble brown and veinéd
He did the pulpit make;
He order'd windows stainéd
Light red and crimson lake.
Sing on, with hymns uproarious,
Ye humble and aloof,
Look up! and oh how glorious
He has restored the roof!

The 'Varsity Students' Rag

I'm afraid the fellows in Putney rather wish they
    had
The social ease and manners of a 'varsity
    undergrad,
For tho' they're awf'lly decent and up to a lark as
    a rule
You want to have the 'varsity touch after a public
    school.

CHORUS:
    We had a rag at Monico's. *We* had a rag at the
        Troc.,
    And the one we had at the Berkeley gave the
        customers quite a shock.
    Then we went to the Popular, and after that—oh
        my!
    I *wish* you'd seen the rag we had in the Grill
        Room at the Cri.

I started a rag in Putney at our Frothblower's
    Branch down there;
We got in a damn'd old lorry and drove to
    Trafalgar Square;

And we each had a couple of toy balloons and
    made a hell of a din,
And I saw a bobby at Parson's Green who looked
    like running us in.

CHORUS: We, etc.

But that's nothing to the rag we had at the college
    the other night;
We'd gallons and gallons of cider—and I got
    frightfully tight.
And then we smash'd up ev'rything, and what was
    the funniest part
We smashed some rotten old pictures which were
    priceless works of art.

CHORUS: We, etc.

There's something about a 'varsity man that
    distinguishes him from a cad:
You can tell by his tie and blazer he's a 'varsity
    undergrad,
And you know that he's always ready and up to a
    bit of a lark,
With a toy balloon and whistle and some cider after
    dark.

CHORUS: We, etc.

The City

Business men with awkward hips
And dirty jokes upon their lips,
And large behinds and jingling chains,
And riddled teeth and riddling brains,
And plump white fingers made to curl
Round some anaemic city girl,
And so lend colour to the lives
And old suspicions of their wives.

Young men who wear on office stools
The ties of minor public schools,
Each learning how to be a sinner
And tell "a good one" after dinner,
And so discover it is rather
Fun to go one more than father.
But father, son and clerk join up
To talk about the Football Cup.

An Eighteenth-Century Calvinistic Hymn

Thank God my Afflictions are such
    That I cannot lie down on my Bed,
And if I but take to my Couch
    I incessantly Vomit and Bleed.

I am not too sure of my Worth,
    Indeed it is tall as a Palm;
But what Fruits can it ever bring forth
    When Leprosy sits at the Helm?

Though Torment's the Soul's Goal's
    Rewards
The contrary's Proof of my Guilt,
While Dancing, Backgammon and Cards,
    Are among the worst Symptoms I've felt.

Oh! I bless the good Lord for my Boils
    For my mental and bodily pains,
For without them my Faith all congeals
    And I'm doomed to HELL'S NE'ER-
    ENDING FLAMES.

For Nineteenth-Century Burials

This cold weather
Carries so many old people away.
Quavering voices and blankets and breath
Go silent together.
The gentle fingers are touching to pray
Which crumple and straighten for Death.
Those cold breezes
Carry the bells away on the air,
Stuttering tales of Gothic, and pass,
Catching new grave flowers into their
    hair,
Beating the chapel and red-coloured
    glass.

Camberley

I wonder whether you would make
A friend of Mrs. Kittiwake?
Colonel Kittiwake, it's true,
Is not the sort of man for you.
I'll tell you how to get to know
Their cosy little bungalow.
When sunset gilds the Surrey pines
The fam'ly usually dines.
So later, in the Surrey dark,
Make for Poonah Punkah Park,
And by the monument to Clive
You'll come to Enniscorthy Drive,
Coolgreena is the last of all,
And mind the terrier when you call.

The drawing-room is done in pink
The other rooms are mauve, I think,
So when you see electric light
Behind pink curtains it's all right.
Knock gently, don't disturb the maid,
She's got to clear, and I'm afraid
That she is less inclined to take
The blame than Mrs. Kittiwake.

Croydon

In a house like that
  Your Uncle Dick was born;
Satchel on back he walked to Whitgift
  Every weekday morn.

Boys together in Coulsdon woodlands,
  Bramble-berried and steep,
He and his pals would look for spadgers
  Hidden deep.

The laurels are speckled in Marchmont
    Avenue
  Just as they were before,
But the steps are dusty that still lead
    up to
  Your Uncle Dick's front door.

Pear and apple in Croydon gardens
  Bud and blossom and fall,
But your Uncle Dick has left his
    Croydon
  Once for all.

Westgate-on-Sea

Hark, I hear the bells of Westgate,
　I will tell you what they sigh,
Where those minarets and steeples
　Prick the open Thanet sky.

Happy bells of eighteen-ninety,
　Bursting from your freestone tower!
Recalling laurel, shrubs and privet,
　Red geraniums in flower.

Feet that scamper on the asphalt
　Through the Borough Council grass,
Till they hide inside the shelter
　Bright with ironwork and glass,

Striving chains of ordered children
　Purple by the sea-breeze made,
Striving on to prunes and suet
　Past the shops on the Parade.

Some with wire around their glasses,
  Some with wire across their teeth,
Writhing frames for running noses
  And the drooping lip beneath.

Church of England bells of Westgate!
  On this balcony I stand,
White the woodwork wriggles round me,
  Clock towers rise on either hand.

For me in my timber arbour
  You have one more message yet,
"Plimsolls, plimsolls in the summer,
  Oh goloshes in the wet!"

The Wykehamist

(To Randolph Churchill, but not about him.)

Broad of Church and broad of mind,
Broad before and broad behind,
A keen ecclesiologist,
A rather dirty Wykehamist.
'Tis not for us to wonder why
He wears that curious knitted tie;
We should not cast reflections on
The very slightest kind of don.
We should not giggle as we like
At his appearance on his bike;
It's something to become a bore,
And more than that, at twenty-four.
It's something too to know your wants
And go full pelt for Norman fonts.
Just now the chestnut trees are dark
And full with shadow in the park,
And "six o'clock!" St. Mary calls
Above the mellow college walls.
The evening stretches arms to twist
And captivate her Wykehamist.

But not for him these autumn days,
He shuts them out with heavy baize;
He gives his Ovaltine a stir
And nibbles at a "petit beurre",
And, satisfying fleshy wants,
He settles down to Norman fonts.

The Sandemanian Meeting-House in Highbury Quadrant

On roaring iron down the Holloway Road
  The red trams and the brown trams pour,
And little each yellow-faced jolted load
  Knows of the fast-shut grained oak door.

From Canonbury, Dalston and Mildmay Park
  The old North London shoots in a train
To the long black platform, gaslit and dark,
  Oh Highbury Station once and again.

Steam or electric, little they care,
  Yellow brick terrace or terra-cotta hall,
White-wood sweet shop or silent square,
  That the LORD OF THE SCRIPTURES IS LORD
    OF ALL.

Away from the barks and the shouts and the
    greetings,
  Psalm-singing over and love-lunch done,
Listening to the Bible in their room for
    meetings,
  Old Sandemanians are hidden from the sun.

The Arrest of Oscar Wilde at the Cadogan Hotel

He sipped at a weak hock and seltzer
  As he gazed at the London skies
Through the Nottingham lace of the curtains
  Or was it his bees-winged eyes?

To the right and before him Pont Street
  Did tower in her new built red,
As hard as the morning gaslight
  That shone on his unmade bed,

"I want some more hock in my seltzer,
  And Robbie, please give me your hand—
Is this the end or beginning?
  How can I understand?

"So you've brought me the latest *Yellow
    Book*:
  And Buchan has got in it now:
Approval of what is approved of
  Is as false as a well-kept vow.

"More hock, Robbie—where is the seltzer?
     Dear boy, pull again at the bell!
They are all little better than *cretins*,
     Though this *is* the Cadogan Hotel.

"One astrakhan coat is at Willis's—
     Another one's at the Savoy:
Do fetch my morocco portmanteau,
     And bring them on later, dear boy."

A thump, and a murmur of voices—
     ("Oh why must they make such a din?")
As the door of the bedroom swung open
     And TWO PLAIN CLOTHES POLICEMEN
          came in:

"Mr. Woilde, we 'ave come for tew take yew
     Where felons and criminals dwell:
We must ask yew tew leave with us quoietly
     For this *is* the Cadogan Hotel."

He rose, and he put down *The Yellow Book*.
     He staggered—and, terrible-eyed,
He brushed past the palms on the staircase
     And was helped to a hansom outside.

Distant View of a Provincial Town

Beside those spires so spick and span
   Against an unencumbered sky
The old Great Western Railway ran
   When someone different was I.

St. Aidan's with the prickly nobs
   And iron spikes and coloured tiles—
Where Auntie Maud devoutly bobs
   In those enriched vermilion aisles:

St. George's where the mattins bell
   But rarely drowned the trams for prayer—
No Popish sight or sound or smell
   Disturbed that gas-invaded air:

St. Mary's where the Rector preached
   In such a jolly friendly way
On cricket, football, things that reached
   The simple life of every day:

And that United Benefice
　With entrance permanently locked,—
How Gothic, grey and sad it is
　Since Mr. Grogley was unfrocked!

The old Great Western Railway shakes
　The old Great Western Railway spins—
The old Great Western Railway makes
　Me very sorry for my sins.

Slough

Come, friendly bombs, and fall on Slough
It isn't fit for humans now,
There isn't grass to graze a cow
  Swarm over, Death!

Come, bombs, and blow to smithereens
Those air-conditioned, bright canteens,
Tinned fruit, tinned meat, tinned milk, tinned
    beans
  Tinned minds, tinned breath.

Mess up the mess they call a town—
A house for ninety-seven down
And once a week a half-a-crown
  For twenty years,

And get that man with double chin
Who'll always cheat and always win,
Who washes his repulsive skin
  In women's tears,

And smash his desk of polished oak
And smash his hands so used to stroke
And stop his boring dirty joke
   And make him yell.

But spare the bald young clerks who add
The profits of the stinking cad;
It's not their fault that they are mad,
   They've tasted Hell.

It's not their fault they do not know
The birdsong from the radio,
It's not their fault they often go
   To Maidenhead

And talk of sports and makes of cars
In various bogus Tudor bars
And daren't look up and see the stars
   But belch instead.

In labour-saving homes, with care
Their wives frizz out peroxide hair
And dry it in synthetic air
   And paint their nails.

Come, friendly bombs, and fall on Slough
To get it ready for the plough.
The cabbages are coming now;
   The earth exhales.

Clash went the Billiard Balls

Clash went the billiard balls in the Clerkenwell
  Social Saloon.
Shut up the shutters and turn down the gas
  they'll be calling the coppers in soon.
Goodnight, Alf!
Goodnight, Bert!
Goodnight, Mrs. Gilligan!
Rain in the archway, no trams in the street.
COP COP
Cop on the cobbleway
Quick little ladylike feet
" 'Ard luck, ain't got a gentleman?"
"Not on a night like this, sweet"
"The Red Lion, Myddleton, all the 'ole lot of
  'em
Shut but a light in The Star
Counting the coppers to see what they've got of
  'em
Glistening wet in the bar
32, 34, 36, 38, Gaskin's not back with 'is tart
Left the 'all door open gives 'himself airs 'e
  does
Thinks 'imself too bloody smart

Gas on in the 'all and it's *we've* got to pay for it
Damn these old stairs and this bug-ridden
    panelling
See 'im to-morrow what *'e's* got to say for it
Get on the bed there and start.''

Love in a Valley

Take me, Lieutenant, to that Surrey homestead!
  Red comes the winter and your rakish car,
Red among the hawthorns, redder than the
    hawberries
  And trails of old man's nuisance, and noisier far.
Far, far below me roll the Coulsdon woodlands,
  White down the valley curves the living rail,[1]
Tall, tall, above me, olive spike the pinewoods,
  Olive against blue-black, moving in the gale.

Deep down the drive go the cushioned
    rhododendrons,
  Deep down, sand deep, drives the heather root,
Deep the spliced timber barked around the
    summer-house,
  Light lies the tennis-court, plantain underfoot.
What a winter welcome to what a Surrey
    homestead!
  Oh! the metal lantern and white enamelled door!
Oh! the spread of orange from the gas-fire on the
    carpet!
  Oh! the tiny patter, sandalled footsteps on the
    floor!

[1] Southern Electric 25 mins.

Fling wide the curtains! – that's a Surrey sunset
    Low down the line sings the Addiscombe train,
Leaded are the windows lozenging the crimson,
    Drained dark the pine in resin-scented rains.
Portable Lieutenant! they carry you to China
    And me to lonely shopping in a brilliant arcade;
Firm hand, fond hand, switch the giddy engine!
    So for us a last time is bright light made.

An Impoverished Irish Peer

Within that parsonage
There is a personage
Who owns a mortgage
  On his Lordship's land,
On his fine plantations,
Well speculated,
With groves of beeches
  On either hand—
On his ten ton schooner
Upon Loch Gowna,
And the silver birches
  Along the land—
Where the little pebbles
Do sing like trebles
As the waters bubble
  Upon the strand—

On his gateway olden
Of plaster moulded
And his splendid carriage way
  To Castle Grand,
(They've been aquatinted
For a book that's printed
And even wanted
  In far England)

His fine saloons there
Would make you swoon, sir,
And each surrounded
  By a gilded band—
And 'tis there Lord Ashtown
Lord Trimlestown and
Clonmore's Lord likewise
  Are entertained.

As many flunkeys
As Finnea has donkeys
Are there at all times
  At himself's command.
Though he doesn't pay them
They all obey him
And would sure die for him
  If he waved his hand;
Yet if His Lordship
Comes for to worship
At the Holy Table
  To take his stand,
Though humbly kneeling
There's no fair dealing
And no kind feeling
  In the parson's hand.
Preaching of Liberty

Also of Charity
In the grand high pulpit
  To see him stand,
You'ld think that personage
In that parsonage
Did own no mortgage
  On His Lordship's land.

Our Padre

Our padre is an old sky pilot,
   Severely now they've clipped his wings,
But still the flagstaff in the Rect'ry garden
   Points to Higher Things.

Still he has got a hearty handshake;
   Still he wears his medals and a stole;
His voice would reach to Heaven, *and* make
   The Rock of Ages Roll.

He's too sincere to join the high church
   Worshipping idols for the Lord,
And, though the lowest church is my
    church,
   Our padre's Broad.

Our padre is an old sky pilot,
   He's tied a reef knot round my heart,
We'll be rocked up to Heaven on a rare old
    tune—
   Come on—take part!

CHORUS

(*Sung*) Pull for the shore, sailor, pull for the
    shore!
  Heed not the raging billow, bend to the
    oar!
Bend to the oar before the padre!
  Proud, with the padre rowing stroke!
Good old padre! God for the services!
  Row like smoke!

Exchange of Livings

Lines suggested by an advertisement in *The Guardian* (the Broad Church newspaper).

The church was locked, so I went to the
    incumbent—
the incumbent enjoying a supine incumbency—
a tennis court, a summerhouse, deckchairs by the
    walnut tree
and only the hum of the bees in the rockery.
"May I have the keys of the church, your
    incumbency?"
"Yes, my dear sir, as a moderate churchman,
I am willing to exchange: light Sunday duty:
    nice district: pop 149: eight hundred per annum:
no extremes: A and M: bicyclist essential:
    same income expected."
"I think I'm the man that you want, your
    incumbency.
Here's my address when I'm not on my bicycle,
    poking about for recumbent stone effigies—
14, Mount Ephraim, Cheltenham, Glos:
Rector St. George-in-the-Rolling Pins, Cripplegate:
non resident pop in the City of London:
eight fifty per annum (but verger an asset):
willing to exchange (no extremes) for incumbency,
similar income, but closer to residence."

Undenominational

Undenominational
　　But still the church of God
He stood in his conventicle
　　And ruled it with a rod.

Undenominational
　　The walls around him rose,
The lamps within their brackets shook
　　To hear the hymns he chose.

"Glory" "Gospel" "Russell Place"
　　"Wrestling Jacob" "Rock"
"Saffron Walden" "Safe at Home"
　　"Dorking" "Plymouth Dock"

I slipped about the chalky lane
　　That runs without the park,
I saw the lone conventicle
　　A beacon in the dark.

Revival ran along the hedge
　　And made my spirit whole
When steam was on the window panes
　　And glory in my soul.

City

When the great bell
BOOMS over the Portland stone urn, and
From the carved cedar wood
Rises the odour of incense,
I SIT DOWN
In St. Botolph Bishopsgate Churchyard
And wait for the spirit of my grandfather
Toddling along from the Barbican.

A Hike on the Downs

"Yes, rub some soap upon your feet!
    We'll hike round Winchester for weeks—
Like ancient Britons—just we two—
    Or more perhaps like ancient Greeks.

"You take your pipe—that will impress
    Your strength on anyone who passes;
I'll take my *Plautus (non purgatus)*
    And both my pairs of horn-rimmed glasses.

"I've got my first, and now I know
    What life is and what life contains—
For, being just a first year man
    You don't meet all the first-class brains.

"Objectively, our Common Room
    Is like a small Athenian State—
Except for Lewis: he's all right
    But do you think he's *quite* first rate?

Hampshire mentality is low,
    And that is why they stare at us.
Yes, here's the earthwork—but it's dark;
    We may as well return by bus."

Dorset

Rime Intrinsica, Fontmell Magna, Sturminster
    Newton and Melbury Bubb,
Whist upon whist upon whist upon whist drive, in
    Institute, Legion and Social Club.
Horny hands that hold the aces which this morning
    held the plough—
While Tranter Reuben, T. S. Eliot, H. G. Wells
    and Edith Sitwell lie in Mellstock Churchyard
    now.

Lord's Day bells from Bingham's Melcombe,
    Iwerne Minister, Shroton, Plush,
Down the grass between the beeches, mellow in the
    evening hush.
Gloved the hands that hold the hymn-book, which
    this morning milked the cow—
While Tranter Reuben, Mary Borden, Brian
    Howard and Harold Acton lie in Mellstock
    Churchyard now.

Light's abode, celestial Salem! Lamps of evening,
    smelling strong,
Gleaming on the pitch-pine, waiting, almost empty
    even-song:

From the aisles each window smiles on grave and
    grass and yew-tree bough—
While Tranter Reuben, Gordon Selfridge, Edna
    Best and Thomas Hardy lie in Mellstock
    Churchyard now.

> NOTE: *The names in the last lines of these stanzas are put in not out of malice or satire but merely for their euphony.*

Calvinistic Evensong

The six bells stopped, and in the dark I heard
Cold silence wait the Calvinistic word;
For Calvin now the soft oil lamps are lit
Hands on their hymnals six old women sit.
Black gowned and sinister, he now appears
Curate-in-charge of aged parish fears.
Let, unaccompanied, that psalm begin
Which deals most harshly with the fruits of sin!
Boy! pump the organ! let the anthem flow
With promise for the chosen saints below!
Pregnant with warning the globed elm trees wait
Fresh coffin-wood beside the churchyard gate.
And that mauve hat three cherries decorate
Next week shall topple from its trembling perch
While wet fields reek like some long empty
    church.

Exeter

The doctor's intellectual wife
  Sat under the ilex tree
The Cathedral bells pealed over the wall
  But never a bell heard she
And the sun played shadowgraphs on her
    book
  Which was writ by A. Huxléy.

Once those bells, those Exeter bells
  Called her to praise and pray
By pink, acacia-shaded walls
  Several times a day
To Wulfric's altar and riddel posts
  While the choir sang Stanford in A.

The doctor jumps in his Morris car,
  The surgery door goes bang,
Clash and whirr down Colleton Crescent,
  Other cars all go hang
My little bus is enough for us—
  Till a tram-car bell went clang.

They brought him in by the big front door
   And a smiling corpse was he;
On the dining-room table they laid him out
   Where the *Bystanders* used to be—
The Tatler, The Sketch and *The Bystander*
For the canons' wives to see.

Now those bells, those Exeter bells
   Call her to praise and pray
By pink, acacia-shaded walls
   Several times a day
To Wulfric's altar and riddel posts
   And the choir sings Stanford in A.

Death of King George V

"New King arrives in his capital by air . . ."
Daily Newspaper.

Spirits of well-shot woodcock, partridge, snipe
 Flutter and bear him up the Norfolk sky:
In that red house in a red mahogany book-case
 The stamp collection waits with mounts long
  dry.

The big blue eyes are shut which saw wrong
  clothing
 And favourite fields and coverts from a horse;
Old men in country houses hear clocks ticking
 Over thick carpets with a deadened force;

Old men who never cheated, never doubted,
 Communicated monthly, sit and stare
At the new suburb stretched beyond the
  run-way
 Where a young man lands hatless from the
  air.

The Heart of Thomas Hardy

The heart of Thomas Hardy flew out of Stinsford
    churchyard
A little thumping fig, it rocketed over the elm
    trees.
Lighter than air it flew straight to where its Creator
Waited in golden nimbus, just as in eighteen sixty,
Hardman and son of Brum had depicted Him in
    the chancel.
Slowly out of the grass, slitting the mounds in the
    centre
Riving apart the roots, rose the new covered
    corpses
Tess and Jude and His Worship, various unmarried
    mothers,
Woodmen, cutters of turf, adulterers, church
    restorers,
Turning aside the stones thump on the upturned
    churchyard.
Soaring over the elm trees slower than Thomas
    Hardy,
Weighted down with a Conscience, now for the first
    time fleshly

Taking form as a growth hung from the feet like a
    sponge-bag.
There, in the heart of the nimbus, twittered the
    heart of Hardy
There, on the edge of the nimbus, slowly revolved
    the corpses
Radiating around the twittering heart of Hardy,
Slowly started to turn in the light of their own
    Creator
Died away in the night as frost will blacken a
    dahlia.

Suicide on Junction Road Station after Abstention from Evening Communion in North London

With the roar of the gas my heart gives a shout—
  To Jehovah Tsidkenu the praise!
Bracket and bracket go blazon it out
  In this Evangelical haze!

Jehovah Jireh! the arches ring,
  The Mintons glisten, and grand
Are the surpliced boys as they sweetly sing
  On the threshold of glory land.

Jehovah Nisi! from Tufnell Park,
  Five minutes to Junction Road,
Through grey brick Gothic and London dark,
  And my sins, a fearful load.

Six on the upside! six on the down side!
  One gaslight in the Booking Hall
And a thousand sins on this lonely station—
  What shall I do with them all?

The Flight from Bootle

Lonely in the Regent Palace,
   Sipping her "Banana Blush",
Lilian lost sight of Alice
   In the honey-coloured rush.

Settled down at last from Bootle,
   Alice whispered, "Just a min,
While I pop upstairs and rootle
   For another safety pin."

Dreamy from the band pavilion
   Drops of the *Immortal Hour*
Fell around the lonely Lilian
   Like an ineffectual shower.

Half an hour she sat and waited
   In the honey-coloured lounge
Till she with herself debated,
   "Time for me to go and scrounge!"

Time enough! or not enough time!
Lilian, you wait in vain;
Alice will not have a rough time,
Nor be quite the same again.

Public House Drunk

Bass   Turn again, Higginson,
Treble   *thrice Mayor of London!*
Bass   Stretch the bow of your bells,
Treble   *St. Mary's steeple!*
Bass   Finsbury, Highbury,
Treble   *you are all undone!*
Bass   Moorfields and Cripplegate,!
Treble   *wake up your people!*

Bass   Saint Andrew Undershaft,
Treble   *Saint Andrew Hubbard,*
Bass   Saint Catherine Coleman,
Treble   *Saint Botolph, Saint Bride's*
Bass   Where are your registers?
Treble   *In vestry cupboard*
Bass   Look him up, Higginson,
Treble   *find where he hides!*

Bass   Out of the Jew's Harp House
Treble   *Old Mother Redcap*

Bass	Turn down the gas again
Treble	*—gas again, Glory!*
Bass	Clean up the bar in the
Treble	*wake of that madcap*
Bass	Lord Mayor of London! Oh
Treble	*Lord what a story!*
Bass	Hold him down, Higginson!
Treble	*send for the beadles!*
Bass	"Fourteen, Macaulay street
Treble	*Bromley-by-Bow*
Bass	Represents pen-nibs
Treble	*steel holders and needles*
Bass	For the Office Equipment
Treble	*Efficiency Co."*

Cheltenham

Floruit, floret, floreat!
  Cheltonia's children cry.
I composed those lines when a summer wind
  Was blowing the elm leaves dry,
And we were seventy-six for seven
  And they had C. B. Fry.

Shall I forget the warm marquee
  And the general's wife so soon,
When my son's colleger[1] acted as tray
  For an ice and a macaroon,
And distant carriages jingled through
  The stuccoed afternoon?

Floruit.   Yes, the Empire Map
  Cheltonia's sons have starred.
Floret.   Still the stream goes on
  Of soldier, brusher[2] and bard.
Floreat.   While behind the limes
  Lengthens the Promenade.

[1] Mortar board.   [2] Schoolmaster.

A Shropshire Lad

N.B.—This should be recited with a Midland accent.
Captain Webb, the swimmer and a relation of Mary
Webb by marriage, was born at Dawley in an industrial
district in Salop.

The gas was on in the Institute,[1]
    The flare was up in the gym,
A man was running a mineral line,
    A lass was singing a hymn,
When Captain Webb the Dawley man,
    Captain Webb from Dawley,
Came swimming along the old canal
    That carried the bricks to Lawley.
    Swimming along—
    Swimming along—
    Swimming along from Severn,
And paying a call at Dawley Bank while
    swimming along to Heaven.

The sun shone low on the railway line
    And over the bricks and stacks,

[1] "The Institute was radiant with gas." Ch. XIX,
Boyhood. A novel in verse by Rev. E. E. Bradford, D.D.

And in at the upstairs windows
  Of the Dawley houses' backs,
When we saw the ghost of Captain Webb,
  Webb in a water sheeting,
Come dripping along in a bathing dress
  To the Saturday evening meeting.
    Dripping along—
    Dripping along—
    To the Congregational Hall;
Dripping and still he rose over the sill and
    faded away in a wall.

There wasn't a man in Oakengates
  That hadn't got hold of the tale,
And over the valley in Ironbridge,
  And round by Coalbrookdale,
How Captain Webb the Dawley man,
  Captain Webb from Dawley,
Rose rigid and dead from the old canal
  That carries the bricks to Lawley.
    Rigid and dead—
    Rigid and dead—
    To the Saturday congregation,
Paying a call at Dawley Bridge on his way to
    his destination.

Upper Lambourne

Up the ash-tree climbs the ivy,
  Up the ivy climbs the sun,
With a twenty-thousand pattering
  Has a valley breeze begun,
Feathery ash, neglected elder,
  Shift the shade and make it run—

Shift the shade toward the nettles,
  And the nettles set it free
To streak the stained Carrara headstone
  Where, in nineteen-twenty-three,
He who trained a hundred winners
  Paid the final Entrance Fee.

Leathery limbs of Upper Lambourne,
  Leathery skin from sun and wind,
Leathery breeches, spreading stables,
  Shining saddles left behind—
To the down the string of horses
  Moving out of sight and mind.

Feathery ash in leathery Lambourne
　　Waves above the sarsen stone,
And Edwardian plantations
　　So coniferously moan
As to make the swelling downland,
　　Far-surrounding, seem their own.

Pot Pourri from a Surrey Garden

Miles of pram in the wind and Pam in the gorse
    track,
  Coco-nut smell of the broom, and a packet of
    Weights
Press'd in the sand. The thud of a hoof on a
    horse-track—
  A horse-riding horse for a horse-track—
  Conifer county of Surrey approached
Through remarkable wrought-iron gates.

Over your boundary now, I wash my face in a
    bird-bath,
  Then which path shall I take! that over there by
    the pram?
Down by the pond! or—yes, I will take the
    slippery third path,
  Trodden away with gym shoes,
  Beautiful fir-dry alley that leads
  To the bountiful body of Pam.

Pam, I adore you, Pam, you great big
    mountainous sports girl,
  Whizzing them over the net, full of the strength
    of five:
That old Malvernian brother, you zephyr and
    khaki shorts girl,
  Although he's playing for Woking,
  Can't stand up
To your wonderful backhand drive.

See the strength of her arm, as firm and hairy
    as Hendren's;
  See the size of her thighs, the pout of her lips
    as, cross,
And full of pent-up strength, she swipes at the
    rhododendrons,
  Lucky the rhododendrons,
  And flings her arrogant love-lock
Back with a petulant toss.

Over the redolent pinewoods, in at the bathroom
    casement,
  One fine Saturday, Windlesham bells shall call:
Up the Butterfield aisle rich with Gothic
    enlacement,
  Licensed now for embracement,
  Pam and I, as the organ
Thunders over you all.

Holy Trinity, Sloane Street

MCMVII

An Acolyte singeth
Light six white tapers with the Flame of Art,
Send incense wreathing to the lily flowers,
And, with your cool hands white,
Swing the warm censer round my bruised heart,
Drop, dove-grey eyes, your penitential showers
On this pale acolyte.

A confirmandus continueth
The tall red house soars upward to the stars,
The doors are chased with sardonyx and gold,
And in the long white room
Thin drapery draws backward to unfold
Cadogan Square between the window-bars
And Whistler's mother knitting in the gloom.

The Priest endeth
How many hearts turn Motherward to-day!
(Red roses faint not on your twining stems!)
Bronze triptych doors unswing!
Wait, restive heart, wait, rounded lips, to pray,

Mid beaten copper interset with gems
Behold! Behold! your King!

On Seeing an Old Poet in the Café Royal

I saw him in the Café Royal.
  Very old and very grand.
Modernistic shone the lamplight
  There in London's fairyland.
"Devilled chicken. Devilled whitebait.
  Devil if I understand.

Where is Oscar? Where is Bosie!
  Have I seen that man before?
And the old one in the corner,
  Is it really Wratislaw!"
Scent of Tutti-Frutti-Sen-Sen
  And cheroots upon the floor.

An Incident in the Early Life of Ebenezer Jones, Poet, 1828

"WE were together at a well-known boarding school of that day (1828), situated at the foot of Highgate Hill, and presided over by a dissenting minister, the Rev. John Bickerdike . . .

We were together, though not on the same form; and on a hot summer afternoon, with about fifty other boys, were listlessly conning our tasks in a large schoolroom built out from the house, which made a cover for us to play under when it was wet. Up the ladder-like stairs from the playground a lurcher dog had strayed into the schoolroom, panting with the heat, his tongue lolling out with thirst. The choleric usher who presided, and was detested by us for his tyranny, seeing this, advanced down the room. Enraged at our attention being distracted from our tasks, he dragged the dog to the top of the stairs, and there lifted him bodily up with the evident intention—and we had known him do similar things—of hurling the poor creature to the bottom.

'YOU SHALL NOT!' rang through the room, as little Ebby, so exclaiming at the top of his voice, rushed with

kindling face to the spot from among all the boys—
some of them twice his age.

But even while the words passed his lips, the heavy
fall was heard, and the sound seemed to travel through
his listening form and face, as, with a strange look of
anguish in one so young, he stood still, threw up his
arms, and burst into an uncontrollable passion of tears.

With a coarse laugh at this, the usher led him back
by his ear to the form; and there he sat, long after his
sobbing had subsided, like one dazed and stunned."
(*From an account of his brother by Sumner Jones in the
1879 re-issue of Ebenezer Jones's "Studies of Sensation
and Event".*)

The lumber of a London-going dray,
The still-new stucco on the London clay,
Hot summer silence over Holloway.

Dissenting chapels, tea-bowers, lovers' lairs,
Neat new-built villas, ample Grecian squares,
Remaining orchards ripening Windsor pears.

Hot silence where the older mansions hide
On Highgate Hill's thick elm-encrusted side,
And Pancras, Hornsey, Islington divide.

June's hottest silence where the hard rays strike
Yon hill-foot house, window and wall alike,
School of the Reverend Mr. Bickerdike,

For sons of Saints, blest with this world's
        possessions
(Seceders from the Protestant Secessions),
Good grounding in the more genteel professions.

A lurcher dog, which draymen kick and pass
Tongue lolling, thirsty over shadeless grass,
Leapt up the playground ladder to the class.

The godly usher left his godly seat,
His skin was prickly in the ungodly heat,
The dog lay panting at his godly feet.

The milkman on the road stood staring in,
The playground nettles nodded "Now begin"—
And Evil waited, quivering, for sin.

He lifted it and not a word he spoke,
His big hand tightened. Could he make it choke
He trembled, sweated, and his temper broke.

"YOU SHALL NOT!" clear across the Highgate Hill
A boy's voice sounded. Creaking forms were still.
The cat jumped slowly from the window sill.

"YOU SHALL NOT!" flat against the summer sun,
Hard as the hard sky frowning over one,
Gloat, little boys! enjoy the coming fun!

"GOD DAMNS A CUR. I AM, I AM HIS WORD!"
He flung it, flung it and it never stirred,
"You shall not!—shall not!" ringing on unheard.

Blind desolation! bleeding, burning rod!
Big, bull-necked Minister of Calvin's God!
Exulting milkman, redfaced, shameless clod,

Look on and jeer! Not Satan's thunder-quake
Can cause the mighty walls of Heaven to shake
As now they do, to hear a boy's heart break.

Trebetherick

We used to picnic where the thrift
   Grew deep and tufted to the edge;
We saw the yellow foam-flakes drift
   In trembling sponges on the ledge
Below us, till the wind would lift
   Them up the cliff and o'er the hedge.
Sand in the sandwiches, wasps in the tea,
Sun on our bathing-dresses heavy with the wet,
Squelch of the bladder-wrack waiting for the sea,
Fleas round the tamarisk, an early cigarette.

From where the coastguard houses stood
   One used to see, below the hill,
The lichened branches of a wood
   In summer silver-cool and still;
And there the Shade of Evil could
   Stretch out at us from Shilla Mill.
Thick with sloe and blackberry, uneven in the
   light,
Lonely ran the hedge, the heavy meadow was
   remote,
The oldest part of Cornwall was the wood as
   black as night,

And the pheasant and the rabbit lay torn open at
   the throat.

But when a storm was at its height,
   And feathery slate was black in rain,
And tamarisks were hung with light
   And golden sand was brown again,
Spring tide and blizzard would unite
   And sea came flooding up the lane.
Waves full of treasure then were roaring up the
   beach,
Ropes round our mackintoshes, waders warm and
   dry,
We waited for the wreckage to come swirling into
   reach,
Ralph, Vasey, Alastair, Biddy, John and I.

Then roller into roller curled
   And thundered down the rocky bay,
And we were in a water-world
   Of rain and blizzard, sea and spray,
And one against the other hurled
   We struggled round to Greenaway.
Blesséd be St. Enodoc, blesséd be the wave,
Blesséd be the springy turf, we pray, pray to
   thee,
Ask for our children all the happy days you gave
To Ralph, Vasey, Alastair, Biddy, John and me.

Oxford: Sudden Illness at the Bus-stop

At the time of evening when cars run sweetly,
  Syringas blossom by Oxford gates.
In her evening velvet with a rose pinned neatly
  By the distant bus-stop a don's wife waits.

From that wide bedroom with its two branched
    lighting
  Over her looking glass, up or down,
When sugar was short and the world was fighting
  She first appeared in velvet gown.

What forks since then have been slammed in
    places?
  What peas turned out from how many a tin?
From plate-glass windows how many faces
  Have watched professors come hobbling in?

Too much, too many! so fetch the doctor,
  This dress has grown such a heavier load
Since Jack was only a Junior Proctor,
  And rents were lower in Rawlinson Road.

Group Life: Letchworth

Tell me Pippididdledum,
  Tell me how the children are.
Working each for weal of all
  After what you said.
Barry's on the common far
  Pedalling the Kiddie Kar.
Ann has had a laxative
  And Alured is dead.
Sympathy is stencilling
  Her decorative leatherwork,
Wilfred's learned a folk-tune for
  The Morris Dancers' band.
I have my ex-Service man and
  Mamie's done a lino-cut.
And Charlie's in the *kinderbank*
  A-kicking up the sand.
Wittle-tittle, wittle-tittle
  Toodle-oodle ducky birds,
What a lot my dicky chicky

Tiny tots have done.
Wouldn't it be jolly now,
    To take our Aertex panters off
And have a jolly tumble in
    The jolly, jolly sun?

Bristol and Clifton

"Yes, I was only sidesman here when last
You came to Evening Communion.
But now I have retired from the bank
I have more leisure time for church finance.
We moved into a somewhat larger house
Than when you knew us in Manilla Road.
This is the window to my lady wife.
You cannot see it now, but in the day
The greens and golds are truly wonderful."

"How very sad. I do not mean about
The window, but I mean about the death
Of Mrs. Battlecock. When did she die?"

"Two years ago when we had just moved in
To Pembroke Road. I rather fear the stairs
And basement kitchen were too much for
      her—
Not that, of course, she did the servants'
      work—
But supervising servants all the day
Meant quite a lot of climbing up and down."

"How very sad. Poor Mrs. Battlecock."
" 'The glory that men do lives after them,'[1]
And so I gave this window in her name.
It's executed by a Bristol firm;
The lady artist who designed it, made
The figure of the lady on the left
Something like Mrs. Battlecock."
"How nice."

            "Yes, was it not? We
had a stained glass window on the stairs at
    home,
In Pembroke Road. But not so good as this.
This window is the glory of the church
At least I think so—and the unstained oak
Looks very chaste beneath it. When I gave
The oak, that brass inscription on your right
Commemorates the fact, the Dorcas Club
Made these blue kneelers, though we do not
    kneel:
We leave that to the Roman Catholics."
"How very nice, indeed. How very nice."

"Seeing I have some knowledge of finance
Our kind Parochial Church Council made

---

[1] Shakespeare, of course.

Me People's Warden, and I'm glad to say
That our collections are still keeping up.
The chancel has been flood-lit, and the stove
Which used to heat the church was obsolete.
So now we've had some radiators fixed
Along the walls and eastward of the aisles;
This last I thought of lest at any time
A Ritualist should be inducted here
And want to put up altars. He would find
The radiators inconvenient.
Our only ritual here is with the Plate;
I think we make it dignified enough.
I take it up myself, and afterwards,
Count the Collection on the vestry safe."

"Forgive me, aren't we talking rather loud?
I think I see a woman praying there."
"Praying? The service is all over now
And here's the verger waiting to turn out
The lights and lock the church up. She cannot
Be Loyal Church of England. Well, good-bye.
Time flies. I must be going. Come again.
There are some pleasant people living here.
I know the Inskips very well indeed."

Sir John Piers

OH! BOLD BAD BARONET
YOU NEED NO CORONET
YOU SIGN YOUR WARRANT WITH
A BLOODY HAND.

INTRODUCTION

"In 1807, Sir John Piers, the last of the name who resided in Tristernagh, and who was a gambler, duellist, and spendthrift, was a schoolfellow of the patriot, Lord Cloncurry. Shortly after the marriage of that nobleman, Piers, who shared his hospitality, and even received pecuniary aid from him, made a diabolical wager to ruin for life the happiness of the wedded pair. Mr. W. J. Fitzpatrick, the able biographer of Lord Cloncurry, says: '. . . A more unlikely person than Lady Cloncurry to prove unfaithful to him she had vowed to love, honour and obey, did not, perhaps, exist in Christendom. Can it be believed that such was the character which Sir John Piers resolved by every art of hell to wither and destroy? A bet, or agreement, as we have heard, was entered into between the monster and some kindred spirit, that in the event of the utter and complete ruin of Lord and Lady Cloncurry's happiness, a sum of money would be placed to the credit of his (Piers') account in a certain Dublin Bank. In case of failure the operation was, of course, to be reversed . . .'

"On the 19th of February, 1807, the celebrated trial, Cloncurry v. Piers, for crim. con., commenced in the Court of King's Bench before Lord Chief Justice Downes. Damages were laid at £100,000. The case created great interest and resulted in a verdict for the plaintiff, £20,000 and costs. John Philpot Curran and Charles Kendal Bushe were the leading Counsel for Lord Cloncurry, and their speeches were what might be expected from such gifted advocates. Those who would wish to read the speeches should consult *Curran and His Contemporaries,* by Charles Philips. Piers put in no appearance at the trial. Haunted by the near approach of retribution, he packed his portmanteau and fled to the Isle of Man. By this proceeding his recognizances became, of course, forfeited to the Crown. After a time the strong arm of the law secured him; he gave what he could reluctantly enough, and his bond for the remainder. Assailed on all sides by creditors, Sir John Piers had a cottage built at Tristernagh, surrounded by a high wall, to protect himself from the minions of justice; but ruin and misfortune overtook him; his estates were sold out in the Encumbered Estates Court." (*Annals of Westmeath, Ancient and Modern,* by James Woods.)

I. The Fête Champêtre

Oh, gay lapped the waves on the shores of Lough
    Ennel
And sweet smelt the breeze 'mid the garlic and
    fennel,
But sweeter and gayer than either of these
Were the songs of the birds in Lord Belvedere's
    trees.

The light skiff is push'd from the weed-waving
    shore,
The rowlocks creak evenly under the oar,
And a boatload of beauty darts over the tide,
The Baron Cloncurry and also his bride.

Lord Belvedere sits like a priest in the prow,
'Tis the Lady Mount Cashel sits next to him now.
And both the de Blacquieres to balance the boat,
Was so much nobility ever afloat?

The party's arranged on the opposite shore,
Lord Clonmore is present and one or two more,
But why has the Lady Cloncurry such fears?
Oh, one of the guests will be Baronet Piers.

The grotto is reached and the parties alight,
The feast is spread out, and begob! what a sight,
Pagodas of jelly in bowls of champagne,
And a tower of blancmange from the Baron
    Kilmaine.

In the shell-covered shelter the grotto affords
The meats and the pies are arranged on the boards,
The nobility laugh and are free from all worry
Excepting the bride of the Baron Cloncurry.

But his lordship is gayer than ever before,
He laughs like the ripples that lap the lake shore,
Nor thinks that his bride has the slightest of fears
Lest one of the guests be the Baronet Piers.

A curricle rolling along on the grass,
The servants make way to allow it to pass,
A high-stepping grey and the wheels flashing yellow
And Sir John in the seat, what a capital fellow!

Huzza for Sir John! and huzza for the fête,
For without his assistance no fête is complete;
Oh, gay is the garland the ladies will wreathe
For the handsomest blade in the County
    Westmeath.

The harness is off with a jingle of steel,
The grey in the grass crops an emerald meal,
Sir John saunters up with a smile and a bow
And the Lady Cloncurry is next to him now.

Her eyes on the landscape, she don't seem to hear
The passing remark he designs for her ear,
For smooth as a phantom and proud as a stork
The Lady Cloncurry continues her walk.

II. The Attempt

I love your brown curls, | black in rain, my
    colleen,
  I love your grey eyes, | by this verdant shore
Two Derravaraghs | to plunge into and drown me,
  Hold not those lakes of | light so near me more.

My hand lies yellow | and hairy in your pink hand,
  Fragilis rubra | of the bramble flower,
Yet soft and thornless, | cool and as caressing
  As grasses bending | heavy with a shower.

See how the clouds twist | over in the twilight,
  See how the gale is | ruffling up the lake;
Lie still for ever | on this little peninsula,
  Heart beat and heart beat | steady till we wake.

Hear how the beech trees | roar above Glencara,
  See how the fungus | circles in the shade,
Roar trees and moan, you | gliding royal daughters,
  Circle us with poison, | we are not afraid.

Gothic on Gothic | my abbey soars around me,
  I've walks and avenues | emerald from rain,
Plentiful timber | in a lake reflected,
  And creamy meadowsweet | scenting my
    demesne.

Press to your cheeks | my hand so hot and wasted,
  Smooth with my fingers | the freckles of your
    frown,
Take you my abbey, | it is yours for always,
  I am so full of | love that I shall drown.

      I lie by the lake water
        And you, Cloncurry, not near,
      I live in a girl's answer,
        You, in a bawd's fear.

III. The Exile

On Mannin's rough coast-line the twilight
  descending
  With its last dying rays on thy height, O Snaefell!
A refuge of dark to the Island is lending
  And to yon *cottage ornée* that lies in the dell.

Its helpless inhabitant dare not appear in
  The rain-weathered streets of adjacent Rumsaa,
But he sees in his dreams the green island of Erin
  And he sits in an orat'ry most of the day.

Yet sometimes, at night, when the waves in
  commotion
  Are tumbling about round the long point of Ayr,
He strides through the tamarisks down to the ocean
  Beyond the lush curraghs of sylvan Lezayre.

Alone with his thoughts when the wild waves
  are beating
  He walks round to Jurby along the wet sand,
And there, where the moon shows the waves are
  retreating,
  He too would retreat to his own native land.

IV. The Return

My speculated avenues are wasted,
  The artificial lake is choked and dry,
My old delight by other lips is tasted,
  Now I can only build my walls and die.

I'll nail the southern wall with Irish peaches,
  Portloman cuttings warmed in silver suns,
And eastwards to Lough Iron's reedy reaches
  I'll build against the vista and the duns.

To westward where the avenue approaches
  Since they have felled the trees of my
    demesne,
And since I'll not be visited by coaches,
  I'll build a mighty wall against the rain.

And from the North, lest you, Malone, should
    spy me,
  You, Sunderlin of Baronstown, the peer,
I'll fill your eye with all the stone that's by
    me
  And live four-square protected in my fear.

Blue dragonflies dart on and do not settle,
  Live things stay not; although my walls are
    high,
They keep not out the knapweed and the
    nettle,
  Stone are my coffin walls, waiting till I die.

V. Tristernagh To-day

In the ivy dusty is the old lock rusty
    That opens rasping on the place of graves,
'Tis no home for mortals behind those portals
    Where the shining dock grows and the nettle
        waves.
Of the walls so ferny, near Tristernagh
        churchyard,
    Often the learned historians write,
And the Abbey splendificent, most
        magnificent,
    Ribbed and springing in ancient night.

Kyrie eleison! blessed St. Bison!
    Holy Piran! Veronica's Veil!
SS. Columb, Colman and St. Attracta,
    Likewise St. Hector, please aid my tale!
Holy Virgin! What's that emergin'?
    I daren't go down in the place of graves,
Head of a dragonfly, twenty times magnified,
    Creeping diagonal, out of the caves!

Dockleaves lapping it, maidenhair flapping it,
  Blue veins mapping it, skin of the moon,
Suck of the bog in it, cold of the frog in it,
  Keep it away from me, shrouded cocoon.
The worms are moving this soft and smooth thing
  And I'm the creature for foolish fears,
There's not a feature that's super nature
  'Tis only rational, 'tis

             SIR
                JOHN
                  PIERS.

Myfanwy

Kind o'er the *kinderbank* leans my Myfanwy,
  White o'er the play-pen the sheen of her dress,
Fresh from the bathroom and soft in the nursery
  Soap-scented fingers I long to caress.

Were you a prefect and head of your dormit'ry?
  Were you a hockey girl, tennis or gym?
Who was your favourite? Who had a crush on you?
  Which were the baths where they taught you to
    swim?

Smooth down the Avenue glitters the bicycle,
  Black-stockinged legs under navy-blue serge,
Home and Colonial, Star, International,
  Balancing bicycle leant on the verge.

Trace me your wheel-tracks, you fortunate bicycle,
  Out of the shopping and into the dark,
Back down the Avenue, back to the pottingshed,
  Back to the house on the fringe of the park.

Golden the light on the locks of Myfanwy,
  Golden the light on the book on her knee,
Finger-marked pages of Rackham's Hans Andersen,
  Time for the children to come down to tea.

Oh! Fuller's angel-cake, Robertson's marmalade,
  Liberty lampshade, come, shine on us all,
My! what a spread for the friends of Myfanwy
  Some in the alcove and some in the hall.

Then what sardines in the half-lighted passages!
  Locking of fingers in long hide-and-seek.
You will protect me, my silken Myfanwy,
  Ringleader, tom-boy, and chum to the weak.

Myfanwy at Oxford

Pink may, double may, dead laburnum
  Shedding an Anglo-Jackson shade,
Shall we ever, my staunch Myfanwy,
  Bicycle down to North Parade?
Kant on the handle-bars, Marx in the
    saddlebag,
  Light my touch on your shoulder-blade.

Sancta Hilda, Myfanwyatia
  Evansensis—I hold your heart,
Willowy banks of a willowy Cherwell a
  Willowy figure with lips apart,
Strong and willowy, strong to pillow me,
  Gold Myfanwy, kisses and art.

Tubular bells of tall St. Barnabas,
  Single clatter above St. Paul,
Chasuble, acolyte, incense-offering,
  Spectacled faces held in thrall.
There in the nimbus and Comper tracery
  Gold Myfanwy blesses us all.

Gleam of gas upon Oxford station,
  Gleam of gas on her straight gold hair,
Hair flung back with an ostentation,
  Waiting alone for a girl friend there.
Second in Mods and a Third in Theology
  Come to breathe again Oxford air.

Her Myfanwy as in Cadena days,
  Her Myfanwy, a schoolgirl voice,
Tentative brush of a cheek in a cocoa crush,
  Coffee and Ulysses, Tennyson, Joyce,
Alpha-minded and other dimensional,
  Freud or Calvary? Take your choice.

Her Myfanwy? *My* Myfanwy.
  Bicycle bells in a Boar's Hill Pine,
Stedman Triple from All Saints' steeple,
  Tom and his hundred and one at nine,
Bells of Butterfield, caught in Keble,
  Sally and backstroke answer *"Mine!"*

Lake District

"On their way back they found the girls at Easedale, sitting beside the cottage where they sell ginger beer in August." (*Peer and Heiress,* Walter Besant.)

I pass the cruet and I see the lake
   Running with light, beyond the garden pine,
   That lake whose waters make me dream her
     mine.
Up to the top board mounting for my sake,
For me she breathes, for me each soft intake,
   For me the plunge, the lake and limbs
     combine.
   I pledge her in non-alcoholic wine
And give the H.P. Sauce another shake.

Spirit of Grasmere, bells of Ambleside,
   Sing you and ring you, water bells, for me;
You water-colour waterfalls may froth.
Long hiking holidays will yet provide
   Long stony lanes and back at six to tea
And Heinz's ketchup on the tablecloth.

In Westminster Abbey

Let me take this other glove off
  As the *vox humana* swells,
And the beauteous fields of Eden
  Bask beneath the Abbey bells.
Here, where England's statesmen lie,
Listen to a lady's cry.

Gracious Lord, oh bomb the Germans.
  Spare their women for Thy Sake,
And if that is not too easy
  We will pardon Thy Mistake.
But, gracious Lord, whate'er shall be,
Don't let anyone bomb me.

Keep our Empire undismembered
  Guide our Forces by Thy Hand,
Gallant blacks from far Jamaica,
  Honduras and Togoland;
Protect them Lord in all their fights,
And, even more, protect the whites.

Think of what our Nation stands for,
    Books from Boots' and country lanes,
Free speech, free passes, class distinction,
    Democracy and proper drains.
Lord, put beneath Thy special care
One-eighty-nine Cadogan Square.

Although dear Lord I am a sinner,
    I have done no major crime;
Now I'll come to Evening Service
    Whensoever I have the time.
So, Lord, reserve for me a crown,
And do not let my shares go down.

I will labour for Thy Kingdom,
    Help our lads to win the war,
Send white feathers to the cowards
    Join the Women's Army Corps,
Then wash the Steps around Thy Throne
In the Eternal Safety Zone.

Now I feel a little better,
    What a treat to hear Thy Word,
Where the bones of leading statesmen.
    Have so often been interr'd.
And now, dear Lord, I cannot wait
Because I have a luncheon date.

Senex

Oh would I could subdue the flesh
  Which sadly troubles me!
And then perhaps could view the flesh
As though I never knew the flesh
  And merry misery.

To see the golden hiking girl
  With wind about her hair,
The tennis-playing, biking girl,
The wholly-to-my-liking girl,
  To see and not to care.

At sundown on my tricycle
  I tour the Borough's edge,
And icy as an icicle
See bicycle by bicycle
  Stacked waiting in the hedge.

Get down from me! I thunder there,
  You spaniels! Shut your jaws!

Your teeth are stuffed with underwear,
Suspenders torn asunder there
    And buttocks in your paws!

Oh whip the dogs away my Lord,
    They make me ill with lust.
Bend bare knees down to pray, my Lord,
Teach sulky lips to say, my Lord,
    That flaxen hair is dust.

Olney Hymns

Oh God the Olney Hymns abound
   With words of Grace which Thou didst
     choose,
And wet the elm above the hedge
   Reflected in the winding Ouse.

Pour in my soul unemptied floods
   That stand between the slopes of clay,
Till deep beyond a deeper depth
   This Olney day is any day.

On a Portrait of a Deaf Man

The kind old face, the egg-shaped head,
  The tie, discreetly loud,
The loosely fitting shooting clothes,
  A closely fitting shroud.

He liked old City dining-rooms,
  Potatoes in their skin,
But now his mouth is wide to let
  The London clay come in.

He took me on long silent walks
  In country lanes when young,
He knew the name of ev'ry bird
  But not the song it sung.

And when he could not hear me speak
  He smiled and looked so wise
That now I do not like to think
  Of maggots in his eyes.

He liked the rain-washed Cornish air
  And smell of ploughed-up soil,
He liked a landscape big and bare
  And painted it in oil.

But least of all he liked that place
  Which hangs on Highgate Hill
Of soaked Carrara-covered earth
  For Londoners to fill.

He would have liked to say good-bye,
  Shake hands with many friends,
In Highgate now his finger-bones
  Stick through his finger-ends.

You, God, who treat him thus and thus,
  Say "Save his soul and pray."
You ask me to believe You and
  I only see decay.

Saint Cadoc

A flame of rushlight in the cell
On holy walls and holy well
And to the west the thundering bay
With soaking seaweed, sand and spray,
  Oh good St. Cadoc pray for me
  Here in your cell beside the sea.

Somewhere the tree, the yellowing oak,
Is waiting for the woodman's stroke,
Waits for the chisel saw and plane
To prime it for the earth again
  And in the earth, for me inside,
  The generous oak tree will have died.

St. Cadoc blest the woods of ash
Bent landwards by the Western lash,
He loved the veinéd threshold stones
Where sun might sometime bleach his
    bones
  He had no cowering fear of death
  For breath of God was Cadoc's breath.

Some cavern generates the germs
To send my body to the worms,
To-day some red hands make the shell
To blow my soul away to Hell
   To-day a pair walks newly married
   Along the path where I'll be carried.

St. Cadoc, when the wind was high,
Saw angels in the Cornish sky
As ocean rollers curled and poured
Their loud Hosannas to the Lord,
   His little cell was not too small
   For that great Lord who made them all.

Here where St. Cadoc sheltered God
The archæologist has trod,
Yet death is now the gentle shore
With Land upon the cliffs before
   And in his cell beside the sea
   The Celtic saint has prayed for me.

Blackfriars

By the shot tower near the chimneys,
  Off the road to Waterloo,
Stands the cottage of "The Agéd"
  As in eighteen-forty-two.
Over brickwork, brownish brickwork,
  Lilac hangs in London sun
And by light fantastic clockwork,
  Moves the drawbridge, sounds the gun.
When the sunset in the side streets
  Brought the breezes up the tide,
Floated bits of daily journals,
  Stable smells and silverside.
And the gaslight, yellow gaslight,
  Flaring in its wiry cage,
Like the Prison Scene in *Norval*
  On the old Olympic stage,
Lit the archway as the thunder,
  And the rumble and the roll,
Heralded a little handcart,
  And "The Agéd" selling coal.

Henley-on-Thames

I see the winding water make
A short and then a shorter lake
    As here stand I,
    And house-boat high
Survey the Upper Thames.
    By sun the mud is amber-dyed
    In ripples slow and flat and wide,
    That flap against the house-boat side
And flop away in gems.

In mud and elder-scented shade
A reach away the breach is made
    By dive and shout
    That circles out
To Henley tower and town;
    And "Boats for Hire" the rafters ring,
    And pink on white the roses cling,
    And red the bright geraniums swing
In baskets dangling down.

When shall I see the Thames again?
The prow-promoted gems again,
  As beefy ATS
  Without their hats
Come shooting through the bridge?
  And "cheerioh" and "cheeri-bye"
  Across the waste of waters die,
  And low the mists of evening lie
And lightly skims the midge.

Parliament Hill Fields

Rumbling under blackened girders, Midland, bound
    for Cricklewood,
Puffed its sulphur to the sunset where that Land of
    Laundries stood.
Rumble under, thunder over, train and tram
    alternate go,
Shake the floor and smudge the ledger,
    Charrington, Dale and Co.,
Nuts and nuggets in the window, trucks along the
    lines below.

When the Bon Marché was shuttered, when the feet
    were hot and tired,
Outside Charrington's we waited, by the "STOP
    HERE IF REQUIRED",
Launched aboard the shopping basket, sat
    precipitately down,
Rocked past Zwanziger the baker's, and the terrace
    blackish brown,
And the curious Anglo-Norman parish church of
    Kentish Town.

Till the tram went over thirty, sighting terminus
    again,
Past municipal lawn tennis and the bobble-hanging
    plane;
Soft the light suburban evening caught our
    ashlar-speckled spire,
Eighteen-sixty Early English, as the mighty elms
    retire
Either side of Brookfield Mansions flashing fine
    French-window fire.

Oh the after-tram-ride quiet, when we heard a mile
    beyond,
Silver music from the bandstand, barking dogs by
    Highgate Pond;
Up the hill where stucco houses in Virginia creeper
    drown—
And my childish wave of pity, seeing children
    carrying down
Sheaves of drooping dandelions to the courts of
    Kentish Town.

A Subaltern's Love-song

Miss J. Hunter Dunn, Miss J. Hunter Dunn,
Furnish'd and burnish'd by Aldershot sun,
What strenuous singles we played after tea,
We in the tournament—you against me!

Love-thirty, love-forty, oh! weakness of joy,
The speed of a swallow, the grace of a boy,
With carefullest carelessness, gaily you won,
I am weak from your loveliness, Joan Hunter
    Dunn.

Miss Joan Hunter Dunn, Miss Joan Hunter
    Dunn,
How mad I am, sad I am, glad that you won.
The warm-handled racket is back in its press,
But my shock-headed victor, she loves me no less.

Her father's euonymus shines as we walk,
And swing past the summer-house, buried in talk,
And cool the verandah that welcomes us in
To the six-o'clock news and a lime-juice and gin.

The scent of the conifers, sound of the bath,
The view from my bedroom of moss-dappled
       path,
As I struggle with double-end evening tie,
For we dance at the Golf Club, my victor and I.

On the floor of her bedroom lie blazer and shorts
And the cream-coloured walls are be-trophied
       with sport,
And westering, questioning settles the sun
On your low-leaded window, Miss Joan Hunter
       Dunn.

The Hillman is waiting, the light's in the hall,
The pictures of Egypt are bright on the wall,
My sweet, I am standing beside the oak stair
And there on the landing's the light on your hair.

By roads "not adopted", by woodlanded ways,
She drove to the club in the late summer haze,
Into nine-o'clock Camberley, heavy with bells
And mushroomy, pine-woody, evergreen smells.

Miss Joan Hunter Dunn, Miss Joan Hunter
       Dunn,
I can hear from the car-park the dance has begun.
Oh! full Surrey twilight! importunate band!
Oh! strongly adorable tennis-girl's hand!

Around us are Rovers and Austins afar,
Above us, the intimate roof of the car,
And here on my right is the girl of my choice,
With the tilt of her nose and the chime of her
    voice,

And the scent of her wrap, and the words never
    said,
And the ominous, ominous dancing ahead.
We sat in the car park till twenty to one
And now I'm engaged to Miss Joan Hunter
    Dunn.

Bristol

Green upon the flooded Avon shone the
    after-storm-wet-sky
Quick the struggling withy branches let the leaves
    of autumn fly
And a star shone over Bristol, wonderfully far and
    high.

Ringers in an oil-lit belfry—Bitton? Kelston? who
    shall say?—
Smoothly practising a plain course, caverned out
    the dying day
As their melancholy music flooded up and ebbed
    away.

Then all Somerset was round me and I saw the
    clippers ride,
High above the moonlit houses, triple-masted on
    the tide,
By the tall embattled church-towers of the Bristol
    waterside.

And an undersong to branches dripping into pools
and wells
Out of multitudes of elm trees over leagues of hills
and dells
Was the mathematic pattern of a plain course on
the bells.*

```
*1  2  2  4  4  5  5  3  3  1  1
 2  1  4  2  5  4  3  5  1  3  2
 3  4  1  5  2  3  4  1  5  2  3
 4  3  5  1  3  2  1  4  2  5  4
 5  5  3  3  1  1  2  2  4  4  5
```

On an Old-Fashioned Water-Colour of Oxford

(Early Twentieth-Century Date)

Shines, billowing cold and gold from Cumnor
    Hurst,
    A winter sunset on wet cobbles, where
    By Canterbury Gate the fishtails flare.
Someone in Corpus reading for a first
Pulls down red blinds and flounders on, immers'd
    In Hegel, heedless of the yellow glare
    On porch and pinnacle and window square,
The brown stone crumbling where the skin has
    burst.

A late, last luncheon staggers out of Peck
    And hires a hansom: from half-flooded grass
    Returning athletes bark at what they see.
But we will mount the horse-tram's upper deck
    And wave salute to Buols', as we pass
    Bound for the Banbury Road in time for tea.

A Lincolnshire Tale

Kirkby with Muckby-cum-Sparrowby-cum-Spinx
Is down a long lane in the county of Lincs,
And often on Wednesdays, well-harnessed and
    spruce,
I would drive into Wiss over Winderby Sluice

A whacking great sunset bathed level and drain
From Kirkby with Muckby to Beckby-on-Bain,
And I saw, as I journeyed, my marketing done
Old Caistorby tower take the last of the sun.

The night air grew nippy. An autumn mist roll'd
(In a scent of dead cabbages) down from the
    wold,
In the ocean of silence that flooded me round
The crunch of the wheels was a comforting
    sound.

The lane lengthened narrowly into the night
With the Bain on its left bank, the drain on its
    right,
And feebly the carriage-lamps glimmered ahead
When all of a sudden *the pony fell dead.*

The remoteness was awful, the stillness intense,
Of invisible fenland, around and immense;
And out of the dark, with a roar and a swell,
Swung, hollowly thundering, Speckleby bell.

Though myself the Archdeacon for many a year,
I had not summoned courage for visiting here;
Our incumbents were mostly eccentric or sad
But—*the Speckleby Rector was said to be mad.*

Oh cold was the ev'ning and tall was the tower
And strangely compelling the tenor bell's power!
As loud on the reed-beds and strong through the
     dark
It toll'd from the church in the tenantless park.

The mansion was ruined, the empty demesne
Was slowly reverting to marshland again—
Marsh where the village was, grass in the Hall,
And the church and the Rectory waiting to fall.

And even in springtime with kingcups about
And stumps of old oak-trees attempting to sprout,
'Twas a sinister place, neither fenland nor wold,
And doubly forbidding in darkness and cold.

As down swung the tenor, a beacon of sound,
Over listening acres of waterlogged ground
I stood by the tombs to see pass and repass
The gleam of a taper, through clear leaded glass,

And such lighting of lights in the thunderous roar
That heart summoned courage to hand at the
    door;
I grated it open on scents I knew well,
The dry smell of damp rot, the hassocky smell.

What a forest of woodwork in ochres and grains
Unevenly doubled in diamonded panes,
And over the plaster, so textured with time,
Sweet discoloration of umber and lime.

The candles ensconced on each high pannelled
    pew
Brought the caverns of brass-studded baize into
    view,
But the roof and its rafters were lost to the sight
As they soared to the dark of the Lincolnshire
    night:

And high from the chancel arch paused to look
    down
A sign-painter's beasts in their fight for the
    Crown,
While massive, impressive, and still as the grave
A three-decker pulpit frowned over the nave.

Shall I ever forget what a stillness was there
When the bell ceased its tolling and thinned on
    the air?
Then an opening door showed a long pair of
    bands
And the Rector himself in his gown and his
    bands.

       ★   ★   ★   ★   ★

Such a fell Visitation I shall not forget,
Such a rush through the dark, that I rush through
    it yet,
And I pray, as the bells ring o'er fenland and hill,
That the Speckleby acres be tenantless still.

St. Barnabas, Oxford

How long was the peril, how breathless the day,
In topaz and beryl, the sun dies away,
His rays lying static at quarter to six
On polychromatical lacing of bricks.
Good Lord, as the angelus floats down the road,
Byzantine St. Barnabas, be Thine Abode.

Where once the fritillaries hung in the grass
A baldachin pillar is guarding the Mass.
Farewell to blue meadows we loved not enough,
And elms in whose shadows were Glanville and
    Clough
Not poets but clergymen hastened to meet
Thy redden'd remorselessness, Cardigan Street.

An Archæological Picnic

In this high pasturage, this Blunden time,
    With Lady's Finger, Smokewort, Lovers' Loss,
And lin-lan-lone a Tennysonian chime
    Stirring the sorrel and the gold-starred moss,
    Cool is the chancel, bright the altar cross.

Drink, Mary, drink your fizzy lemonade
    And leave the king-cups; take your grey felt hat;
Here, where the low-side window lends a shade,
    There, where the key lies underneath the mat,
    The rude forefathers of the hamlet sat.

Sweet smell of cerements and of cold wet stones,
    Hassock and cassock, paraffin and pew;
Green in a light which that sublime Burne-Jones
    White-hot and wondering from the glass-kiln
        drew,
    Gleams and re-gleams this Trans arcade anew.

So stand you waiting, freckled innocence!
    For me the squinch and squint and Trans arcade;
For you, where meadow grass is evidence,
    With flattened pattern, of our picnic made,
    One bottle more of fizzy lemonade.

May-Day Song for North Oxford

(Annie Laurie Tune)

Belbroughton Road is bonny, and pinkly bursts the
    spray
Of prunus and forsythia across the public way,
For a full spring-tide of blossom seethed and
    departed hence,
Leaving land-locked pools of jonquils by sunny
    garden fence.

And a constant sound of flushing runneth from
    windows where
The toothbrush too is airing in this new North
    Oxford air
From Summerfields to Lynam's, the thirsty tarmac
    dries,
And a Cherwell mist dissolveth on elm-discovering
    skies.

Oh! well-bound Wells and Bridges! Oh! earnest
    ethical search
For the wide high-table λογος of St. C. S. Lewis's
    Church.

This diamond-eyed Spring morning my soul soars
    up the slope
Of a right good rough-cast buttress on the
    housewall of my hope.

And open-necked and freckled, where once there
    grazed the cows,
Emancipated children swing on old apple boughs,
And pastel-shaded book rooms bring New Ideas to
    birth
As the whitening hawthorn only hears the heart
    beat of the earth.

Before Invasion, 1940

Still heavy with may, and the sky ready to fall,
Meadows buttercup high, shed and chicken and
    wire?
And here where the wind leans on a sycamore silver
    wall,
Are you still taller than sycamores, gallant Victorian
    spire?

Still, fairly intact, and demolishing squads about,
Bracketed station lamp with your oil-light taken
    away?
Weep flowering currant, while your bitter cascades
    are out,
Born in an age of railways, for flowering into
    to-day!

Ireland with Emily

Bells are booming down the bohreens,
  White the mist along the grass.
Now the Julias, Maeves and Maureens
  Move between the fields to Mass.
Twisted trees of small green apple
Guard the decent whitewashed chapel,
Gilded gates and doorway grained
Pointed windows richly stained
  With many-coloured Munich glass.

See the black-shawled congregations
  On the broidered vestment gaze
Murmur past the painted stations
  As Thy Sacred Heart displays
Lush Kildare of scented meadows,
Roscommon, thin in ash-tree shadows,
And Westmeath the lake-reflected,
Spreading Leix the hill-protected,
  Kneeling all in silver haze?

In yews and woodbine, walls and guelder,
  Nettle-deep the faithful rest,

Winding leagues of flowering elder,
Sycamore with ivy dressed,
Ruins in demesnes deserted,
Bog-surrounded bramble-skirted—
Townlands rich or townlands mean as
These, oh, counties of them screen us
  In the Kingdom of the West.

Stony seaboard, far and foreign,
  Stony hills poured over space,
Stony outcrop of the Burren,
  Stones in every fertile place,
Little fields with boulders dotted,
Grey-stone shoulders saffron-spotted,
Stone-walled cabins thatched with reeds,
Where a Stone Age people breeds
  The last of Europe's stone age race.

Has it held, the warm June weather?
  Draining shallow sea-pools dry,
When we bicycled together
  Down the bohreens fuchsia-high.
Till there rose, abrupt and lonely,
A ruined abbey, chancel only,
Lichen-crusted, time befriended,
Soared the arches, splayed and splendid,
  Romanesque against the sky.

There in pinnacled protection,
  One extinguished family waits
A Church of Ireland resurrection
  By the broken, rusty gates.
Sheepswool, straw and droppings cover,
Graves of spinster, rake and lover,
Whose fantastic mausoleum
Sings its own seablown Te Deum,
  In and out the slipping slates.

Margate, 1940

From out the Queen's Highcliffe for weeks at a
    stretch
I watched how the mower evaded the vetch,
So that over the putting-course rashes were seen
Of pink and of yellow among the burnt green.

How restful to putt, when the strains of a band
Announced a *thé dansant* was on the Grand,
While over the privet, comminglingly clear,
I heard lesser "Co-Optimists" down by the pier.

How lightly municipal, meltingly tarr'd,
Were the walks through the Laws by the Queen's
    Promenade
As soft over Cliftonville languished the light
Down Harold Road, Norfolk Road, into the night.

Oh! then what a pleasure to see the ground floor
With tables for two laid as tables for four,
And bottles of sauce and Kia-Ora[1] and squash
Awaiting their owners who'd gone up to wash—

[1] Pronounced "Kee-Ora".

Who had gone up to wash the ozone from their
    skins
The sand from their legs and the Rock from their
    chins,
To prepare for an evening of dancing and cards
And forget the sea-breeze on the dry promenades.

From third floor and fourth floor the children
    looked down
Upon ribbons of light in the salt-scented town;
And drowning the trams roared the sound of the
    sea
As it washed in the shingle the scraps of their tea.

★　　★　　★　　★　　★

Beside the Queen's Highcliffe now rank grows the
    vetch,
Now dark is the terrace, a storm-battered stretch;
And I think, as the fairy-lit sights I recall,
It is those we are fighting for, foremost of all.

Invasion Exercise on the Poultry Farm

Softly croons the radiogram, loudly hoot the owls,
Judy gives the door a slam and goes to feed the
    fowls.
Marty rolls a Craven A around her ruby lips
And runs her yellow fingers down her corduroyded
    hips,
Shuts her mouth and screws her eyes and puffs her
    fag alight
And hears some most peculiar cries that echo
    through the night.
Ting-a-ling the telephone, to-whit to-whoo the owls,
Judy, Judy, Judy girl, and have you fed the fowls?
No answer as the poultry gate is swinging there
    ajar.
Boom the bombers overhead, between the clouds a
    star,
And just outside, among the arks, in a shadowy
    sheltered place
Lie Judy and a paratroop in horrible embrace.
Ting-a-ling the telephone. "Yes, this is Marty
    Hayne."
"Have you seen a paratroop come walking down
    your lane?

He may be on your premises, he may be
    somewhere near,
And if he is report the fact to Major Maxton-
    Weir."
Marty moves in dread towards the window—standing
    there
Draws the curtain—sees the guilty movement of the
    pair. [1]
White with rage and lined with age but strong
    and sturdy still
Marty now co-ordinates her passions and her will,
She will teach that Judy girl to trifle with her heart
And go and kiss a paratroop like any common tart.
She switches up the radiogram and covered by the
    blare
She goes and gets a riding whip and whirls it in the
    air,
She fetches down a length of rope and rushes,
    breathing hard
To let the couple have it for embracing in the yard.
Crack! the pair are paralysed. Click! they cannot
    stir.
Zip! she's trussed the paratroop. There's no
    embracing *her.*
"Hullo, hullo, hullo, hullo . . . Major
    Maxton-Weir?
I've trussed your missing paratroop. He's waiting
    for you here."

[1] These lines in italic are by Henry Oscar.

The Planster's Vision

Cut down that timber! Bells, too many and
  strong,
    Pouring their music through the branches bare,
    From moon-white church-towers down the
      windy air
Have pealed the centuries out with Evensong.
Remove those cottages, a huddled throng!
    Too many babies have been born in there,
    Too many coffins, bumping down the stair,
Carried the old their garden paths along.

I have a Vision of The Future, chum,
    The workers' flats in fields of soya beans
    Tower up like silver pencils, score on score:
And Surging Millions hear the Challenge come
    From microphones in communal canteens
    "No Right! No Wrong! All's perfect,
      evermore."

In a Bath Teashop

"Let us not speak, for the love we bear one
    another—
  Let us hold hands and look."
She, such a very ordinary little woman:
  He, such a thumping crook;
But both, for a moment, little lower than the
    angels
  In the teashop's ingle-nook.

Before the Anæsthetic,
or
A Real Fright

Intolerably sad, profound
St. Giles's bells are ringing round,
They bring the slanting summer rain
To tap the chestnut boughs again
Whose shadowy cave of rainy leaves
The gusty belfry-song receives.
Intolerably sad and true,
Victorian red and jewel* blue,
The mellow bells are ringing round
And charge the evening light with sound,
And I look motionless from bed
On heavy trees and purple red
And hear the midland bricks and tiles
Throw back the bells of stone St. Giles,
Bells, ancient now as castle walls,
Now hard and new as pitchpine stalls,
Now full with help from ages past,
Now dull with death and hell at last.

*Adjective from Rumer Godden.

Swing up! and give me hope of life,
Swing down! and plunge the surgeon's knife.
I, breathing for a moment, see
Death wing himself away from me
And think, as on this bed I lie,
Is it extinction when I die?
I move my limbs and use my sight;
Not yet, thank God, not yet the Night.
Oh better far those echoing hells
Half-threaten'd in the pealing bells
Than that this "I" should cease to be—
Come quickly, Lord, come quick to me.
St. Giles's bells are asking now
"And hast thou known the Lord, hast
      thou?"
St. Giles's bells, they richly ring
"And was that Lord our Christ the King?"
St. Giles's bells they hear me call
I never knew the Lord at all.
Oh not in me your Saviour dwells
You ancient, rich St. Giles's bells.
Illuminated missals—spires—
Wide screens and decorated quires—
All these I loved, and on my knees
I thanked myself for knowing these
And watched the morning sunlight pass
Through richly stained Victorian glass
And in the colour-shafted air

I, kneeling, thought the Lord was there.
Now, lying in the gathering mist
I know that Lord did not exist;
Now, lest this "I" should cease to be,
Come, real Lord, come quick to me.
With every gust the chestnut sighs,
With every breath, a mortal dies;
The man who smiled alone, alone,
And went his journey on his own
With "Will you give my wife this letter,
In case, of course, I don't get better?"
Waits for his coffin lid to close
On waxen head and yellow toes.
Almighty Saviour, had I Faith
There'd be no fight with kindly Death.
Intolerably long and deep
St. Giles's bells swing on in sleep:
"But still you go from here alone"
Say all the bells about the Throne.

On Hearing the Full Peal of Ten Bells from Christ Church, Swindon, Wilts.

Your peal of ten ring over then this town,
Ring on my men nor ever ring them down.
This winter chill, let sunset spill cold fire
On villa'd hill and on Sir Gilbert's spire,
So new, so high, so pure, so broach'd, so tall.
Long run the thunder of the bells through all!

Oh still white headstones on these fields of
    sound
Hear you the wedding joybells wheeling round?
Oh brick-built breeding boxes of new souls,
Hear how the pealing through the louvres rolls!
Now birth and death-reminding bells ring clear,
Loud under 'planes and over changing gear.

Youth and Age on Beaulieu River, Hants

Early sun on Beaulieu water
  Lights the undersides of oaks,
Clumps of leaves it floods and blanches,
All transparent glow the branches
  Which the double sunlight soaks;
To her craft on Beaulieu water
Clemency the General's daughter
  Pulls across with even strokes.

Schoolboy-sure she is this morning;
  Soon her sharpie's rigg'd and free.
Cool beneath a garden awning
  Mrs. Fairclough, sipping tea
And raising large long-distance glasses
As the little sharpie passes,
  Sighs our sailor girl to see:

Tulip figure, so appealing,
  Oval face, so serious-eyed,

Tree-roots pass'd and muddy beaches,
On to huge and lake-like reaches,
   Soft and sun-warm, see her glide—
Slacks the slim young limbs revealing,
Sun-brown arm the tiller feeling—
  With the wind and with the tide.

Evening light will bring the water,
  Day-long sun will burst the bud,
Clemency, the General's daughter,
  Will return upon the flood.
But the older woman only
Knows the ebb-tide leaves her lonely
  With the shining fields of mud.

East Anglian Bathe

Oh when the early morning at the seaside
  Took us with hurrying steps from Horsey
    Mere
To see the whistling bent-grass on the leeside
  And then the tumbled breaker-line appear,
On high, the clouds with mighty adumbration
  Sailed over us to seaward fast and clear
And jellyfish in quivering isolation
  Lay silted in the dry sand of the breeze
And we, along the table-land of beach blown
  Went gooseflesh from our shoulders to our
    knees
And ran to catch the football, each to each
    thrown,
  In the soft and swirling music of the seas.

There splashed about our ankles as we waded
  Those intersecting wavelets morning-cold,
And sudden dark a patch of sea was shaded,
  And sudden light, another patch would hold
The warmth of whirling atoms in a sun-shot

And underwater sandstorm green and gold.
So in we dived and louder than a gunshot
   Sea-water broke in fountains down the ear.
How cold the bathe, how chattering cold the
      drying,
   How welcoming the inland reeds appear,
The wood-smoke and the breakfast and the
      frying,
   And your warm freshwater ripples, Horsey
      Mere.

Sunday Afternoon Service in
St. Enodoc Church, Cornwall

Come on! come on! This hillock hides the spire,
Now that one and now none. As winds about
The burnished path through lady's finger,
    thyme
And bright varieties of saxifrage,
So grows the tinny tenor faint or loud
And all things draw towards St. Enodoc.

Come on! come on! and it is five to three.

Paths, unfamiliar to golfers' brogues,
Cross the eleventh fairway broadside on
And leave the fourteenth tee for thirteenth
    green,
Ignoring Royal and Ancient, bound for God.
  Come on! come on! no longer bare of foot,
The sole grows hot in London shoes again.
Jack Lambourne in his Sunday navy-blue
Wears tie and collar, all from Selfridge's.
There's Enid with a silly parasol,
And Graham in gray flannel with a crease

Across the middle of his coat which lay
Pressed 'neath the box of his Meccano set,
Sunday to Sunday.
        Still, Come on! come on!
The tinny tenor. Hover-flies remain
More than a moment on a ragwort bunch,
And people's passing shadows don't disturb
Red Admirals basking with their wings apart.
  A mile of sunny, empty sand away,
A mile of shallow pools and lugworm casts,
Safe, faint and surfy, laps the lowest tide.
  Even the villas have a Sunday look.
The Ransom mower's locked into the shed.
"I have a splitting headache from the sun,"
And bedroom windows flutter cheerful chintz
Where, double-aspirined, a mother sleeps;
While father in the loggia reads a book,
Large, desultory, birthday-present size,
Published with colour plates by *Country Life*,
A Bernard Darwin on *The English Links*
Or Braid and Taylor on *The Mashie Shot*.
Come on! come on! he thinks of Monday's
    round—
Come on! come on! that interlocking grip!
Come on! come on! he drops into a doze—

Come on! come on! more far and far away
The children climb a final stile to church;
Electoral Roll still flapping in the porch—
Then the cool silence of St. Enodoc.

My eyes, recovering in the sudden shade,
Discern the long-known little things within—
A map of France in damp above my pew,
Grey-blue of granite in the small arcade
(Late Perp: and not a Parker specimen
But roughly hewn on windy Bodmin Moor),
The modest windows palely glazed with green,
The smooth slate floor, the rounded wooden
      roof,
The Norman arch, the cable-moulded font—
All have a humble and West Country look.
Oh "drastic restoration" of the guide!
Oh three-light window by a Plymouth firm!
Absurd, truncated screen! oh sticky pews!
Embroidered altar-cloth! untended lamps!
So soaked in worship you are loved too well
For that dispassionate and critic stare
That I would use beyond the parish bounds
Biking in high-banked lanes from tower to
      tower
On sunny, antiquarian afternoons.

Come on! come on! a final pull. Tom Blake
Stalks over from the bell-rope to his pew
Just as he slopes about the windy cliffs
Looking for wreckage in a likely tide,
Nor gives the Holy Table glance or nod.
A rattle as red baize is drawn aside,
Miss Rhoda Poulden pulls the tremolo,
The oboe, flute and vox humana stops;
A Village Voluntary fills the air
And ceases suddenly as it began,
Save for one oboe faintly humming on,
As slow the weary clergyman subsides
Tired with his bike-ride from the parish church.
He runs his hands once, twice, across his face
"Dearly beloved . . . " and a bumble-bee
Zooms itself free into the churchyard sun
And so my thoughts this happy Sabbathtide.
  Where deep cliffs loom enormous, where
    cascade
Mesembryanthemum and stone-crop down,
Where the gull looks no larger than a lark
Hung midway twixt the cliff-top and the sand,
Sun-shadowed valleys roll along the sea.
Forced by the backwash, see the nearest wave
Rise to a wall of huge, translucent green

And crumble into spray along the top
Blown seaward by the land-breeze. Now she
    breaks
And in an arch of thunder plunges down
To burst and tumble, foam on top of foam,
Criss-crossing, baffled, sucked and shot again,
A waterfall of whiteness, down a rock,
Without a source but roller's furthest reach:
And tufts of sea-pink, high and dry for years,
Are flooded out of ledges, boulders seem
No bigger than a pebble washed about
In this tremendous tide. Oh kindly slate!
To give me shelter in this crevice dry.
These shivering stalks of bent-grass, lucky
    plant,
Have better chance than I to last the storm.
Oh kindly slate of these unaltered cliffs,
Firm, barren substrate of our windy fields!
Oh lichened slate in walls, they knew your
    worth
Who raised you up to make this House of God
What faith was his, that dim, that Cornish saint,
Small rushlight of a long-forgotten church,
Who lived with God on this unfriendly shore,
Who knew He made the Atlantic and the stones
And destined seamen here to end their lives
Dashed on a rock, rolled over in the surf,

And not one hair forgotten. Now they lie
In centuries of sand beside the church.
Less pitiable are they than the corpse
Of a large golfer, only four weeks dead,
This sunlit and sea-distant afternoon;
"Praise ye the Lord!" and in another key
The Lord's name by harmonium be praised,
"The Second Evening and the Fourteenth
Psalm."

The Irish Unionist's Farewell to Greta Hellstrom in 1922

Golden haired and golden hearted
    I would ever have you be,
As you were when last we parted
    Smiling slow and sad at me.
Oh! the fighting down of passion!
    Oh! the century-seeming pain—
Parting in this off-hand fashion
    In Dungarvan in the rain.

Slanting eyes of blue, unweeping,
    Stands my Swedish beauty where
Gusts of Irish rain are sweeping
    Round the statue in the square;
Corner boys against the walling
    Watch us furtively in vain,
And the Angelus is calling
    Through Dungarvan in the rain.

Gales along the Commeragh Mountains,
    Beating sleet on creaking signs,

Iron gutters turned to fountains,
  And the windscreen laced with lines,
And the evening getting later,
  And the ache—increased again,
As the distance grows the greater
  From Dungarvan in the rain.

There is no one now to wonder
  What eccentric sits in state
While the beech trees rock and thunder
  Round his gate-lodge and his gate.
Gone—the ornamental plaster,
  Gone—the overgrown demesne
And the car goes fast, and faster,
  From Dungarvan in the rain.

Had I kissed and drawn you to me,
  Had you yielded warm for cold,
What a power had pounded through me
  As I stroked your streaming gold!
You were right to keep us parted:
  Bound and parted we remain,
Aching, if unbroken hearted—
  Oh! Dungarvan in the rain!

In Memory of Basil, Marquess of Dufferin and Ava

On such a morning as this
   with the birds ricocheting their music
Out of the whelming elms
   to a copper beech's embrace
And a sifting sound of leaves
   from multitudinous branches
Running across the park
   to a chequer of light on the lake,
On such a morning as this
   with *The Times* for June the eleventh
Left with coffee and toast
   you opened the breakfast-room window
And, sprawled on the southward terrace,
   Said: "That means war in September."

Friend of my youth, you are dead!
   and the long peal pours from the steeple
Over this sunlit quad
   in our University city

And soaks in Headington stone.
  Motionless stand the pinnacles.
Under the flying sky
  as though they too listened and waited
Like me for your dear return
  with a Bullingdon noise of an evening
In a Sports-Bugatti from Thame
  that belonged to a man in Magdalen.
Friend of my youth, you are dead!
  and the quads are empty without you.

Then there were people about.
  Each hour, like an Oxford archway,
Open on long green lawns
  and distant unvisited buildings
And you my friend were explorer
  and so you remained to me always
Humorous, reckless, loyal—
  my kind, heavy-lidded companion.
Stop, oh many bells, stop
  pouring on roses and creeper
Your unremembering peal
  this hollow, unhallowed V.E. day,—
I am deaf to your notes and dead
  by a soldier's body in Burma.

South London Sketch, 1944

From Bermondsey to Wandsworth
   So many churches are,
Some with apsidal chancels,
   Some Perpendicular
And schools by E. R. Robson
   In the style of Norman Shaw
Where blue-serged adolescence learn'd
   To model and to draw.

Oh, in among the houses,
   The viaduct below,
Stood the Coffee Essence Factory
   Of Robinson and Co.
Burnt and brown and tumbled down
   And done with years ago
Where the waters of the Wandle do
   Lugubriously flow.

From dust of dead explosions,
  From scarlet-hearted fires,
All unconcerned this train draws in
  And smoothly that retires
And calmly rise on smoky skies
  Of intersected wires
The Nonconformist spirelets
  And the Church of England spires.

South London Sketch, 1844

Lavender Sweep is drowned in Wandsworth,
  Drowned in jessamine up to the neck,
Beetles sway upon bending grass leagues
  Shoulder-level to Tooting Bec.
Rich as Middlesex, rich in signboards,
  Lie the lover-trod lanes between,
Red Man, Green Man, Horse and Waggoner,
  Elms and sycamores round a green.
Burst, good June, with a rush this morning,
  Bindweed weave me an emerald rope
Sun, shine bright on the blossoming trellises,
  June and lavender, bring me hope.

Indoor Games near Newbury

In among the silver birches winding ways of tarmac
    wander
  And the signs to Bussock Bottom, Tussock Wood
    and Windy Brake,
Gabled lodges, tile-hung churches, catch the lights
    of our Lagonda
  As we drive to Wendy's party, lemon curd and
    Christmas cake.

  Rich the makes of motor whirring,
  Past the pine-plantation purring
    Come up, Hupmobile, Delage!
  Short the way your chauffeurs travel,
  Crunching over private gravel
    Each from out his warm garáge.

Oh but Wendy, when the carpet yielded to my
    indoor pumps
  There you stood, your gold hair streaming,
  Handsome in the hall-light gleaming
There you looked and there you led me off into the
    game of clumps

Then the new Victrola playing
And your funny uncle saying
"Choose your partners for a fox-trot! Dance until
    it's *tea* o'clock!
    "Come on, young 'uns, foot it featly!"
Was it chance that paired us neatly,
I, who loved you so completely,
You, who pressed me closely to you, hard against
    your party frock?

"Meet me when you've finished eating!" So we
    met and no one found us.
    Oh that dark and furry cupboard while the
    rest played hide and seek!
Holding hands our two hearts beating in the
    bedroom silence round us,
    Holding hands and hardly hearing sudden
    footstep, thud and shriek.

Love that lay too deep for kissing—
"Where *is* Wendy? Wendy's missing!
Love so pure it *had* to end,
Love so strong that I was frighten'd
When you gripped my fingers tight and
Hugging, whispered "I'm your friend."

Good-bye Wendy! Send the fairies, pinewood elf
    and larch tree gnome,

Spingle-spangled stars are peeping
At the lush Lagonda creeping
Down the winding ways of tarmac to the leaded
   lights of home.

There, among the silver birches,
All the bells of all the churches
Sounded in the bath-waste running out into the
   frosty air.
Wendy speeded my undressing,
Wendy is the sheet's caressing
Wendy bending gives a blessing,
Holds me as I drift to dreamland, safe inside my
   slumberwear.

St. Saviour's, Aberdeen Park, Highbury, London, N.

With oh such peculiar branching and over-reaching
    of wire
  Trolley-bus standards pick their threads from the
    London sky
Diminishing up the perspective, Highbury-bound
    retire
  Threads and buses and standards with plane trees
    volleying by
And, more peculiar still, that ever-increasing spire
  Bulges over the housetops, polychromatic and
    high.

Stop the trolley-bus stop! And here, where the
    roads unite
  Of weariest worn-out London—no cigarettes, no
    beer,
No repairs undertaken, nothing in stock—alight;
  For over the waste of willow-herb, look at her,
    sailing clear,
A great Victorian church, tall, unbroken and bright

In a sun that's setting in Willesden and saturating
   us here.

These were the streets my parents knew when they
      loved and won—
   The brougham that crunched the gravel, the
   laurel-girt paths that wind,
Geranium-beds for the lawn, Venetian blinds for
      the sun,
   A separate tradesman's entrance, straw in the
   mews behind,
Just in the four-mile radius where hackney carriages
      run,
   Solid Italianate houses for the solid commercial
   mind.

These were the streets they knew; and I, by
      descent, belong
   To these tall neglected houses divided into flats.
Only the church remains, where carriages used to
      throng
   And my mother stepped out in flounces and my
   father stepped out in spats
To shadowy stained-glass matins or gas-lit evensong
   And back in a country quiet with doffing of
   chimney hats.

Great red church of my parents, cruciform crossing
      they knew—
   Over these same encaustics they and their parents
   trod

Bound through a red-brick transept for a once
familiar pew
Where the organ set them singing and the sermon
let them nod
And up this coloured brickwork the same long
shadows grew
As these in the stencilled chancel where I kneel
in the presence of God.

Wonder beyond Time's wonders, that Bread so
white and small
Veiled in golden curtains, too mighty for men to
see,
Is the Power which sends the shadows up this
polychrome wall,
Is God who created the present, the
chain-smoking millions and me;
Beyond the throb of the engines is the throbbing
heart of all—
Christ, at this Highbury altar, I offer myself To
Thee.

Beside the Seaside

Green Shutters, shut your shutters! Windyridge,
Let winds unnoticed whistle round your hill!
High Dormers, draw your curtains! Slam the
    door,
And pack the family in the Morris eight.
Lock up the garage. Put her in reverse,
Back out with care, now, forward, off—away!
The richer people living farther out
O'ertake us in their Rovers. We, in turn,
Pass poorer families hurrying on foot
Towards the station. Very soon the town
Will echo to the groan of empty trams
And sweetshops advertise Ice Cream in vain.
Solihull, Headingley and Golders Green.
Preston and Swindon, Manchester and Leeds,
Braintree and Bocking, hear the sea! the sea!
The smack of breakers upon windy rocks,
Spray blowing backwards from their curling walls
Of green translucent water. England leaves
Her centre for her tide-line. Father's toes,

Though now encased in coloured socks and shoes
And pressing the accelerator hard,
Ache for the feel of sand and little shrimps
To tickle in between them. Mother vows
To be more patient with the family:
Just for its sake she will be young again.
And, at that moment, Jennifer is sick
(Over-excitement must have brought it on,
The hurried breakfast and the early start)
And Michael's rather pale, and as for Ann . . .
"Please stop a moment, Hubert, anywhere."
   So evening sunlight shows us Sandy Cove
The same as last year and the year before.
Still on the brick front of the Baptist Church
SIX-THIRTY. PREACHER:—*Mr. Pentecost*—
All visitors are welcomed. Still the quartz
Glitters along the tops of garden walls.
Those macrocarpa still survive the gales
They must have had last winter. Still the shops
Remain unaltered on the Esplanade—
The Circulating Library, the Stores,
Jill's Pantry, Cynthia's Ditty Box (Antiques),
Trecarrow (Maps and Souvenirs and Guides).
Still on the terrace of the big hotel

Pale pink hydrangeas turn a rusty brown
Where sea winds catch them, and yet do not die.
The bumpy lane between the tamarisks,
The escallonia hedge, and still it's there—
Our lodging-house, ten minutes from the shore.
Still unprepared to make a picnic lunch
Except by notice on the previous day.
Still nowhere for the children when it's wet
Except that smelly, overcrowded lounge,
And still no garage for the motor-car.
Still on the bedroom wall, the list of rules:
Don't waste the water. It is pumped by hand.
Don't throw old blades into the W.C.
Don't keep the bathroom long and don't be late
For meals and don't hang swim-suits out on sills
(A line has been provided at the back).
Don't empty children's sand-shoes in the hall.
Don't this, Don't that. Ah, still the same, the same
    same
As it was last year and the year before—
But rather more expensive, now, of course.
"Anne, Jennifer and Michael—run along
Down to the sands and find yourselves some
    friends
While Dad and I unpack." The sea! the sea!
  On a secluded corner of the beach

A game of rounders has been organized
By Mr. Pedder, schoolmaster and friend
Of boys and girls—particularly girls.
And here it was the tragedy began,
That life-long tragedy to Jennifer
Which ate into her soul and made her take
To secretarial work in later life
In a department of the Board of Trade.
See boys and girls assembled for the game.
Reflected in the rock pools, freckled legs
Hop, skip and jump in coltish ecstasy.
Ah! parted lips and little pearly teeth,
Wide eyes, snub noses, shorts, divided skirts!
And last year's queen of them was Jennifer.
The snubbiest, cheekiest, lissomest of all.
One smile from her sent Mr. Pedder back
Contented to his lodgings. She could wave
Her little finger and the elder boys
Came at her bidding. Even tiny Ruth,
Old Lady D'Erncourt's grandchild, pet of all,
Would bring her shells as timid offerings.
So now with Anne and Michael see her stand,
Our Jennifer, our own, our last year's queen,
For this year's *début* fully confident.

"Get in your places." Heard above the waves
Are Mr. Pedder's organizing shouts.
"Come on. Look sharp. The tide is coming in!"
"He hasn't seen me yet," thinks Jennifer.
"Line up your team behind you, Christabel!"
On the wet sea-sand waiting to be seen
She stands with Anne and Michael. Let him turn
And then he'll see me. Let him only turn.
Smack went the tennis ball. The bare feet ran.
And smack again. "He's out! Well caught,
    Delphine!"
Shrieks, cartwheels, tumbling joyance of the
    waves.
Oh Mr. Pedder, look! Oh here I am!
And there the three of them forlornly stood.
"You ask him, Jennifer." "No—Michael?—
    Anne?"
"I'd rather not." "Fains I." "It's up to you."
"Oh, very well, then." Timidly she goes,
Timid and proud, for the last time a child.
"Can *we* play, Mr. Pedder?" But his eyes
Are out to where, among the tousled heads,
He sees the golden curls of Christabel.
"Can *we* play, Mr. Pedder?" So he turns.
"*Who* have we here?" The jolly, jolly voice,
The same but not the same. "*Who* have we here?
The Rawlings children! Yes, of course, you may,

Join that side, children, under Christabel."
No friendly wallop on the B.T.M.
No loving arm-squeeze and no special look.
Oh darting heart-burn, *under Christabel!*
So all those holidays the bitter truth
Sank into Jennifer. No longer queen.
She had outgrown her strength, as Mummy said,
And Mummy made her wear these spectacles.
Because of Mummy she had lost her looks.
Had lost her looks? Still she was Jennifer.
The sands were still the same, the rocks the same,
The seaweed-waving pools, the bathing-cove,
The outline of the cliffs, the times of tide.
And I'm the same, of course I'm always ME
But all that August those terrific waves
Thundered defeat along the rocky coast,
And ginger-beery surf hissed 'Christabel!'
   Enough of tragedy! Let wail of gulls,
The sunbows in the breakers and the breeze
Which blows the sand into the sandwiches,
Let castles crumbling in the rise of tide,
Let cool dank caves and dark interstices
Where, underneath the squelching bladderwrack,
Lurk stinging fin and sharp, marauding claw

Ready to pierce the rope-soled bathing-shoe,
Let darting prawn and helpless jelly-fish
Spell joy or misery to youth. For we,
We older ones, have thoughts of higher things.
Whether we like to sit with Penguin books
In sheltered alcoves farther up the cliff,
Or to eat winkles on the Esplanade,
Or to play golf along the crowded course,
Or on a twopenny borough council chair
To doze away the strains of *Humoresque*,
Adapted for the cornet and the drums
By the conductor of the Silver Band,
Whether we own a tandem or a Rolls,
Whether we Rudge it or we trudge it, still
A single topic occupies our minds.
'Tis hinted at or boldly blazoned in
Our accents, clothes and ways of eating fish,
And being introduced and taking leave,
'Farewell,' 'So long,' 'Bunghosky,' 'Cheeribye'—
That topic all-absorbing, as it was,
Is now and ever shall be, to us—CLASS.
   Mr. and Mrs. Stephen Grosvenor-Smith
(He manages a Bank in Nottingham)
Have come to Sandy Cove for thirty years

And now they think the place is going down.
   "Not what it was, I'm very much afraid.
Look at that little mite with *Attaboy*
Printed across her paper sailor hat.
Disgusting, isn't it? Who *can* they be,
Her parents, to allow such forwardness?"
   The Browns, who thus are commented upon,
Have certainly done very well indeed.
The elder children bringing money in,
Father still working; with allowances
For this and that and little income-tax,
They probably earn seven times as much
As poor old Grosvenor-Smith. But who will
        grudge
Them this, their wild, spontaneous holiday?
The morning paddle, then the mystery tour
By motor-coach inland this afternoon.
For that old mother what a happy time!
At last past bearing children, she can sit
Reposeful on a crowded bit of beach.
A week of idleness, the salty winds
Play in her greying hair; the summer sun
Puts back her freckles so that Alfred Brown
Remembers courting days in Gospel Oak
And takes her to the Flannel Dance to-night.

But all the same they think the place 'Stuck up'
And Blackpool, next year—if there *is* a next.
  And all the time the waves, the waves, the
    waves
Chase, intersect and flatten on the sand
As they have done for centuries, as they will
For centuries to come, when not a soul
Is left to picnic on the blazing rocks,
When England is not England, when mankind
Has blown himself to pieces. Still the sea,
Consolingly disastrous, will return
While the strange starfish, hugely magnified,
Wait in the jewelled basin of a pool.

North Coast Recollections

No people on the golf-links, not a crack
Of well-swung driver from the fourteenth tee,
No sailing bounding ball across the turf
And lady's slipper of the fairway. Black
Rises Bray Hill and, Stepper-wards, the sun
Sends Bray Hill's phantom stretching to the
  church.
The lane, the links, the beach, the cliffs are
  bare
The neighbourhood is dressing for a dance
And lamps are being lit in bungalows.
  O! thymy time of evening: clover scent
And feathery tamarisk round the churchyard
  wall
And shrivelled sea-pinks and this foreshore pale
With silver sand and sharpened quartz and slate
And brittle twigs, bleached, salted and prepared
For kindling blue-flamed fires on winter nights.
  Here Petroc landed, here I stand to-day;
The same Atlantic surges roll for me
As rolled for Parson Hawker and for him,
And spent their gathering thunder on the rocks

Crashing with pebbly backwash, burst again
And strewed the nibbled fields along the cliffs.

When low tides drain the estuary gold
Small intersecting breakers far away
Ripple about a bar of shifting sand
Where centuries ago were weaving woods
Where centuries hence, there will be woods
    again.

Within the bungalow of Mrs. Hanks
Her daughter Phoebe now French-chalks the
    floor.
Norman and Gordon in their dancing pumps
Slide up and down, but can't make concrete
    smooth.
"My Sweet Hortense . . ."
Sings louder down the garden than the sea.
"A practice record, Phoebe. Mummykins,
Gordon and I will do the washing-up."
"We picnic here; we scrounge and help
    ourselves,"
Says Mrs. Hanks, and visitors will smile
To see them all turn to it. Boys and girls
Weed in the sterile garden, mostly sand
And dead tomato-plants and chicken-runs.
To-day they cleaned the dulled Benares ware
(Dulled by the sea-mist), early made the beds,
And Phoebe twirled the icing round the cake

And Gordon tinkered with the gramophone
While into an immense enamel jug
Norman poured "Eiffel Tower" for lemonade.
 O! healthy bodies, bursting into 'teens
And bursting out of last year's summer clothes,
Fluff barking and French windows banging to
Till the asbestos walling of the place
Shakes with the life it shelters, and with all
The preparations for this evening's dance.

Now drains the colour from the convolvulus,
The windows of Trenain are flashing fire,
Black sways the tamarisk against the West,
And bathing things are taken in from sills.
One child still zig-zags homewards up the lane,
Cold on bare feet he feels the dew-wet sand.
Behind him, from a walk along the cliff,
Come pater and the mater and the dogs.

 Four macrocarpa hide the tennis club.
Two children of a chartered actuary
(Beaworthy, Trouncer, Heppelwhite and Co.),
Harold and Bonzo Trouncer are engaged
In semi-finals for the tournament.
"Love thirty!" Pang! across the evening air

Twangs Harold's racquet. Plung! the ball
    returns.
Experience at Budleigh Salterton
Keeps Bonzo steady at the net. "Well done!"
"Love forty!" Captain Mycroft, midst applause,
Pronounces for the Trouncers, to be sure
He can't be certain Bonzo didn't reach
A shade across the net, but Demon Sex,
That tulip figure in white cotton dress,
Bare legs, wide eyes and so tip-tilted nose
Quite overset him. Harold serves again
And Mrs. Pardon says it's getting cold,
Miss Myatt shivers, Lady Lambourn thinks
These English evenings are a little damp
And dreams herself again in fair Shanghai.
"Game . . .AND! and thank you!"; so the pair
    from Rock
(A neighbouring and less exclusive place)
Defeated, climb into their Morris Ten.
"The final is to-morrow! Well, good night!"
  He lay in wait, he lay in wait, he did,
John Lambourn, curly-headed; dewy grass
Dampened his flannels, but he still remained.
The sunset drained the colours black and gold,
From his all-glorious First Eleven scarf.
But still he waited by the twilit hedge.

Only his eyes blazed blue with early love,
Blue blazing in the darkness of the lane,
Blue blazer, less incalculably blue,
Dark scarf, white flannels, supple body still,
First love, first light, first life. A heartbeat
  noise!
His heart or little feet? A snap of twigs
Dry, dead and brown the under branches part
And Bonzo scrambles by their secret way.
First love so deep, John Lambourn cannot
  speak,
So deep, he feels a tightening in his throat,
So tender, he could brush away the sand
Dried up in patches on her freckled legs,
Could hold her gently till the stars went down,
And if she cut herself would staunch the
  wound,
Yes, even with his First Eleven scarf,
And hold it there for hours.
So happy, and so deep he loves the world,
Could worship God and rocks and stones and
  trees,
Be nicer to his mother, kill himself
If that would make him pure enough for her.
And so at last he manages to say
"You going to the Hanks's hop to-night?"
"Well, I'm not sure. Are you?" "I think I
  may—
"It's pretty dud though,—only lemonade."

Sir Gawaint was a right and goodly knight
Nor ever wist he to uncurtis be.
So old, so lovely, and so very true!
Then Mrs. Wilder shut the Walter Crane
And tied the tapes and tucked her youngest in
What time without amidst the lavender
At late last 'He' played Primula and Prue
With new-found liveliness; for bed was soon.
And in the garage, serious seventeen
Harvey, the eldest, hammered on, content,
Fixing a mizzen to his model boat.
"Coo-ee! Coo-ee!" across the lavender,
Across the mist of pale gypsophila
And lolling purple poppies, Mumsie called,
A splendid sunset lit the rocking-horse
And Morris pattern of the nursery walls.
"Coo-ee!" the slate-hung, goodly-builded house
And sunset-sodden garden fell to quiet.
"Prue! Primsie! Mumsie wants you.
    Sleepi-byes!"
Prue jumped the marigolds and hid herself,
Her sister scampered to the Wendy Hut
And Harvey, glancing at his Ingersoll,
Thought "Damn! I must get ready for the
    dance."

So on this after-storm-lit evening
To Jim the raindrops in the tamarisk,
The fuchsia bells, the sodden matchbox lid
That checked a tiny torrent in the lane
Were magnified and shining clear with life.
Then pealing out across the estuary
The Padstow bells range up for practice-night
An undersong to birds and dripping shrubs.
The full Atlantic at September spring
Flooded a final tide-mark up the sand,
And ocean sank to silence under bells,
And the next breaker was a lesser one
Then lesser still. Atlantic, bells and birds
Were layer on interchanging layers of sound.

A Lincolnshire Church

Greyly tremendous the thunder
Hung over the width of the wold
But here the green marsh was alight
In a huge cloud cavern of gold,
And there, on a gentle eminence,
Topping some ash trees, a tower
Silver and brown in the sunlight,
Worn by sea-wind and shower,
Lincolnshire Middle Pointed.
And around it, turning their backs,
The usual sprinkle of villas;
The usual woman in slacks,
Cigarette in her mouth,
Regretting Americans, stands
As a wireless croons in the kitchen
Manicuring her hands.
Dear old, bloody old England
Of telegraph poles and tin,
Seemingly so indifferent

And with so little soul to win.
What sort of church, I wonder?
The path is a grassy mat,
And grass is drowning the headstones
Sloping this way and that.
"Cathedral Glass" in the windows,
A roof of unsuitable slate—
Restored with a vengeance, for certain,
About eighteen-eighty-eight.
The door swung easily open
(Unlocked, for these parts, is odd)
And there on the South aisle altar
Is the tabernacle of God.
There where the white light flickers
By the white and silver veil,
A wafer dipped in a wine-drop
Is the Presence the angels hail,
Is God who created the Heavens
And the wide green marsh as well
Who sings in the sky with the skylark
Who calls in the evening bell,
Is God who prepared His coming
With fruit of the earth for his food
With stone for building His churches

And trees for making His rood.
There where the white light flickers,
Our Creator is with us yet,
To be worshipped by you and the woman
Of the slacks and the cigarette.

*   *   *   *   *

The great door shuts, and lessens
That roar of churchyard trees
And the Presence of God Incarnate
Has brought me to my knees.
"I acknowledge my transgressions"
The well-known phrases rolled
With thunder sailing over
From the heavily clouded wold.
"And my sin is ever before me."
There in the lighted East
He stood in that lowering sunlight,
An Indian Christian priest.
And why he was here in Lincolnshire
I neither asked nor knew,
Nor whether his flock was many
Nor whether his flock was few
I thought of the heaving waters
That bore him from sun glare harsh

Of some Indian Anglican Mission
To this green enormous marsh.
There where the white light flickers,
Here, as the rains descend,
The same mysterious Godhead
Is welcoming His friend.

The Town Clerk's Views

"Yes, the Town Clerk will see you." In I went.
He was, like all Town Clerks, from north of Trent;
A man with bye-laws busy in his head
Whose Mayor and Council followed where he led.
His most capacious brain will make us cower,
His only weakness is a lust for power—
And that is not a weakness, people think,
When unaccompanied by bribes or drink.
So let us hear this cool careerist tell
His plans to turn our country into hell.
"I cannot say how shock'd I am to see
The *variations* in our scenery.
Just take for instance, at a casual glance,
Our muddled coastline opposite to France:
Dickensian houses by the Channel tides
With old hipp'd roofs and weather-boarded sides.
I blush to think one corner of our isle
Lacks concrete villas in the modern style.
Straight lines of hops in pale brown earth of Kent,
Yeomen's square houses once, no doubt, content

With willow-bordered horse-pond, oast-house, shed,
Wide orchard, garden walls of browny-red—
All useless now, but what fine sites they'ld be
For workers' flats and some light industry.
Those lumpy church towers, unadorned with spires,
And wavy roofs that burn like smouldering fires
In sharp spring sunlight over ashen flint
Are out of date as some old aquatint.
Then glance below the line of Sussex downs
To stucco terraces of seaside towns
Turn'd into flats and residential clubs
Above the wind-slashed Corporation shrubs.
Such Georgian relics should by now, I feel,
Be all rebuilt in glass and polished steel.
Bournemouth is looking up. I'm glad to say
That modernistic there has come to stay.
I walk the asphalt paths of Branksome Chine
In resin-scented air like strong Greek wine
And dream of cliffs of flats along those heights,
Floodlit at night with green electric lights.
But as for Dorset's flint and Purbeck stone,
Its old thatched farms in dips of down alone—
It should be merged with Hants and made to be
A self-contained and plann'd community.
Like Flint and Rutland, it is much too small

And has no reason to exist at all.
Of Devon one can hardly say the same,
But "South-West Area One" 's a better name
For those red sandstone cliffs that stain the sea
By mid-Victoria's Italy—Torquay.
And "South-West Area Two" could well include
The whole of Cornwall from Land's End to Bude.
Need I retrace my steps through other shires?
Pinnacled Somerset? Northampton's spires?
Burford's broad High Street is descending still
Stone-roofed and golden-walled her elmy hill
To meet the river Windrush. What a shame
Her houses are not brick and all the same.
Oxford is growing up to date at last.
Cambridge, I fear, is living in the past.
She needs more factories, not useless things
Like that great chapel which they keep at King's.
As for remote East Anglia, he who searches
Finds only thatch and vast, redundant churches.
But that's the dark side. I can safely say
A beauteous England's really on the way.
Already our hotels are pretty good
For those who're fond of *very simple food*—
Cod and two veg., free pepper, salt and mustard,

Followed by nice hard plums and lumpy custard,
A pint of bitter beer for one-and-four,
Then coffee in the lounge a shilling more.
In a few years this country will be looking
As uniform and tasty as its cooking.
Hamlets which fail to pass the planners' test
Will be demolished. We'll rebuild the rest
To look like Welwyn mixed with Middle West.
All fields we'll turn to sports grounds, lit at night
From concrete standards by fluorescent light:
And over all the land, instead of trees,
Clean poles and wire will whisper in the breeze.
We'll keep one ancient village just to show
What England once was when the times were
    slow—
Broadway for me. But here I know I must
Ask the opinion of our National Trust.
And ev'ry old cathedral that you enter
By then will be an Area Culture Centre.
Instead of nonsense about Death and Heaven
Lectures on civic duty will be given;
Eurhythmic classes dancing round the spire,
And economics courses in the choir.
So don't encourage tourists. Stay your hand
Until we've really got the country plann'd."

Index of First Lines

177

179

Index of Places and Counties